Life Skills

for autistic adolescents

Aliki Kassotaki - Speech Language Pathologist MSc, BSc

SOCIAL STEPS

Upbility Publications LTD | 81–83 Grivas Digenis Avenue, Nicosia, 1090 Cyprus

E-mail: info@upbility.eu

www.upbility.net

SKU: EN-EB1133

Author: Aliki Kassotaki – Speech-Language Pathologist MSc, BSc

ABOUT

AUTHOR

ALIKI
KASSOTAKI

Writing is a solitary affair, and that's something I enjoy most of the time. Of course, I equally enjoy the company of my young and older students. I started working as a speech therapist in 2000. Thirteen years later, I wrote the first remedial manual. I wanted to share the knowledge and personal experience I have gained over the years. I have not stopped writing since then, and at the same time, I continue to practice my profession. One complements the other. The children show me the way, and I join them in easy and challenging paths.

With empathy, humility, knowledge, and respect, I continue with my motto:

"Young children, fresh with uncluttered minds, the world before them – to what treasures will you lead them?"

Gladys M. Hunt

UPBILITY PUBLICATIONS
www.upbility.net

CONTENTS

CONTENTS

Bibliography

- Anderson, Luke. Life Skills for Autistic Teens: Preparing for a Full and Productive Life. Autism Asperger Publishing Company, 2014.
- Attwood, Tony. The Complete Guide to Asperger's Syndrome. Jessica Kingsley Publishers, 2007.
- Baker, Jed. Social Skills Training for Children and Adolescents with Asperger Syndrome and Social-Communication Problems. Autism Asperger Publishing Company, 2003.
- Chasson, Gregory S., et al. Manualized Cognitive Behavioral Therapy for Youth with Autism Spectrum Disorder: A Comprehensive Clinician's Guide. Springer, 2018.
- Clements, Jeanette, and Paul Brooks. Practical Solutions for Educating Young Children with High-Functioning Autism and Asperger Syndrome. Autism Asperger Publishing Company, 2002.
- Grandin, Temple, and Sean Barron. The Unwritten Rules of Social Relationships: Decoding Social Mysteries Through the Unique Perspectives of Autism. Future Horizons, 2005.
- Gray, Carol. The New Social Story Book. Future Horizons, 2010.
- Laugeson, Elizabeth A. The Science of Making Friends: Helping Socially Challenged Teens and Young Adults. Jossey-Bass, 2013.
- Myles, Brenda Smith. The Hidden Curriculum: Practical Solutions for Understanding Unstated Rules in Social Situations. AAPC Publishing, 2004.
- Ozonoff, Sally, et al. Evidence-Based Psychotherapies for Children and Adolescents. Guilford Press, 2016.
- Reaven, Judy. Group Interventions for Children with Autism Spectrum Disorders: A Focus on Social Competence and Anxiety Reduction. Guilford Press, 2012.
- Rotheram-Fuller, Erin, et al. Adolescents with Autism Spectrum Disorder: The Cognitive Behavioral Therapy Approach. Springer, 2014.
- Sicile-Kira, Chantal. Adolescents on the Autism Spectrum: A Parent's Guide to the Cognitive, Social, Physical, and Transition Needs of Teenagers with Autism Spectrum Disorders. Penguin, 2006.
- Sofronoff, Kate, et al. Social Skills Training: For Children and Adolescents with Asperger Syndrome and Social-Communication Problems. AAPC Publishing, 2004.
- Storch, Eric A., et al. CBT for Anxiety Disorders: A Practitioner Book. Guilford Press, 2016.
- Volker, Martin A., et al. Behavioral and Emotional Disorders in Adolescents: Nature, Assessment, and Treatment. Guilford Press, 2010.
- White, Susan W. Social Skills Training for Adolescents with Autism Spectrum Disorder: Evidence-Based Practices for Behavioral Interventions. Norton, 2011.
- Williams, Kari Dunn. The Social Skills Picture Book: Teaching Play, Emotion, and Communication to Children with Autism. Future Horizons, 2001.
- Winner, Michelle Garcia. Thinking About You, Thinking About Me. Think Social Publishing, 2007.
- Wood, Jeffrey J., et al. Cognitive Behavioral Therapy for Adult Asperger Syndrome. Guilford Press, 2013.

Life Skills

Life skills are basic abilities that enable individuals to effectively and independently manage different aspects of everyday life. They encompass a wide range of competencies that help people to manage personal affairs, interact with others, and cope with everyday challenges.

Basic life skills:

Communication skills: Verbal and non-verbal communication, active listening, assertiveness.
Importance: Facilitates clear expression, mutual understanding, and healthy relationships.

Interpersonal skills: Relationship building, empathy, teamwork, conflict resolution.
Importance: Strengthens social interactions and support networks.

Decision-making and problem-solving: Critical thinking, situational analysis, making informed choices.
Importance: Enables effective handling of challenges and opportunities.

Self-management: Time management, goal setting, self-discipline.
Importance: Promotes productivity, personal development, and stress management.

Adaptability and flexibility: Coping with change, stress management, resilience.
Importance: Helps manage uncertainties and life transitions smoothly.

Financial control: Money management, saving, investing.
Importance: Ensures financial stability and planning for the future.

Health and wellness: Nutrition, exercise, mental health, self-care.
Importance: Maintains physical and mental well-being.

Practical and everyday living skills: Household management, personal hygiene, basic household tasks.
Importance: Supports independent living and responsibility.

How to use this book

The book's content includes scenarios, exercises, and practical guidelines to enhance the communication and social skills of autistic adolescents.

1. Planning the intervention

- **Goal setting:** Set clear and realistic goals according to the adolescent's needs.
- **Select materials:** Select the exercises and scenarios that match the intervention goals from the book.

2. Conducting the intervention

- **Be flexible:** Adapt activities to suit each adolescent's individual needs and pace.
- **Create a safe environment:** Ensure the therapy environment is supportive and secure for the adolescent.
- **Encourage participation:** Encourage the adolescent to participate and express their opinions and feelings actively.

3. Integrating skills into everyday life

- **Realistic scenarios:** Use scenarios that reflect real-life situations to help the adolescent apply the skills they learn.
- **Practical application:** Provide opportunities for the adolescent to practice new skills in a safe and structured environment.

4. Feedback and Evaluation

- **Monitor progress:** Record the adolescent's progress and discuss the results of each session with them.
- **Continuous feedback:** Ask the adolescent for feedback on the exercises and activities they found useful and interesting.
- **Review the plan:** Adjust the treatment plan based on the adolescent's progress and needs.

5. Working with family and school

- **Communication:** Keep the family and school informed about the adolescent's goals and progress.
- **Collaboration:** Work with family and teachers to ensure a coherent approach to the adolescent's skills development.

1

Starting and maintaining a conversation

Useful tips

Story

In a similar situation:

Start with something simple: You can ask something commonplace like "How are you?" or "How was your day?" It's an effective way to start a conversation.

Use common interests: If you know someone interested in something you like, talk about it. For example, if you both like video games, start a conversation about your favorite video game.

Ask for opinion or advice: You can ask something like "What do you think about...?" or "Can you recommend a good book about...?"

Keep the conversation interesting: Show interest in what others are saying and ask additional questions based on their answers. For example, if they talk about a hobby, ask how they started it or what they like best about it.

Use positive body language: Try to be friendly and smile when you speak. It shows the other person that you enjoy the conversation.

End the conversation positively: When the conversation ends, you can say something like "It was great talking to you. Let's do it again sometime!" That can leave a good impression.

Nick stands next to two friends who are having a conversation. He wants to join but finds it difficult to engage or maintain participation.

- What do you think about what happened to Nick?
- Can you describe his feelings?
- How do you think the story progresses?
- Have you ever had similar feelings?

1

Objectives:	Activities:

#1

Recognizing and expressing feelings

Learn to recognize and express their feelings.

- **Emotion cards:** Create cards with pictures of people expressing different emotions (joy, sadness, anger, anxiety, surprise). Ask the adolescent to identify and describe the emotion they see.
- **Daily emotions journal:** Ask the adolescent to keep a journal in which they write down their feelings daily and describe what made them feel that way.

#2

Role-playing and simulations

Enhance their social skills through practice.

- **Role-playing game:** Create scenarios that resemble Nick's story. For example, play the role of Nick, who wants to participate in the conversation. Allow the adolescent to try different ways to initiate and sustain a conversation.
- **Simulating everyday situations:** Prepare several everyday life scenarios (e.g., asking for help, asking a question) and ask the adolescent to act them out.

#3

Developing conversational skills

Learn how to start and maintain a conversation.

- **Conversation starter cards:** Create cards with questions that can be used to start a conversation (e.g., How was your day?).
- **Listening exercise:** Play the game "Yes, and..." where one person starts a sentence, and the other has to continue by saying "Yes, and..." That helps strengthen listening skills and learn how to continue the conversation.

#4

Using positive body language

Learn to identify and use positive body language.

- **Observation and imitation:** Show videos with positive body language (smiles, eye contact, open posture). Ask the adolescent to observe and imitate these behaviors.
- **Mirror:** Use a mirror for the adolescent to practice positive body language and facial expressions.

#5

Maintaining conversation and interest

Learn to show interest and keep the conversation lively.

- **Question game:** Play the game in which one person asks questions, and the other has to answer and respond with a question. That helps to enhance interactivity and keep the conversation going.
- **Focusing on common interests:** Find out together what the adolescent likes and create conversations around these topics.

#6

Ending a conversation

Learn how to end a conversation in a positive way.

- **Simulating conversation endings:** Create scenarios where the conversation comes to an end and ask the adolescent to say something positive to end it (e.g. It was nice talking to you!).

1

Treatment plan

Situation	Feelings	Automatic thoughts	Evidence supporting these thoughts	Evidence against these thoughts	Alternative thoughts	Behavioral response
I want to join the discussion, but I find it difficult. ___ ___ ___ ___ ___ ___ ___ ___	Restless, nervous, isolated ___ ___ ___ ___ ___ ___ ___ ___ ___ ___	I don't know what to say. They don't want me to participate. I'll say something stupid. ___ ___ ___ ___ ___ ___	I couldn't think of anything to say last time. ___ ___ ___ ___ ___ ___ ___ ___	I can have comfortable conversations with my friends. ___ ___ ___ ___ ___ ___ ___	I could ask a question about what they say. My friends like me and accept me. ___ ___ ___ ___ ___	Listen carefully, find a point of interest and ask a relevant question. Use active listening to show interest. ___ ___ ___

Identifying the situation:

Identify specific situations where they find it difficult to participate in the conversation.

Feelings:

Write down their feelings during these situations.

Automatic thoughts:

Identify their immediate thoughts about what may prevent them from participating.

Evidence supporting these thoughts:

Identify why they made these thoughts.

Evidence against these thoughts:

Think about why these thoughts may be false.

Alternative thoughts:

Develop positive and constructive thoughts to replace the negative ones.

Behavioral response:

Plan specific actions for participating in the conversation, such as asking questions or using active listening techniques.

2

Non-verbal cues

Useful tips

In a similar situation:

Direct questions: When unsure, it's okay to ask directly about the other person's feelings or thoughts. For example, "I'm not sure I understand how you're feeling right now. Can you tell me more?"

Observation: Pay attention to the discussed topic, context, and tone of voice. All of these can help decode feelings.

Study: Learn about the basic signs of body language. Understanding common gestures, postures, and facial expressions can help to interpret the emotions and intentions of others better.

Repetition: Repeat what the other person said to show them you understood. It not only lets them confirm that you understood but also allows them to clarify if there is a misunderstanding.

Feedback: After social interactions, ask a trusted friend for feedback on the expressive cues given and how they were dealt with. That can help identify specific areas for improvement.

Mindfulness: Engage in mindfulness exercises to enhance focus and awareness during conversations.

Story

Mary has difficulty understanding facial expressions that show emotions, such as sadness or discomfort, reacting in ways that seem irrelevant to the situation. Despite the challenges, she tries to improve by utilizing direct communication and her friends' patience.

- Can you describe how Mary feels?
- Have you ever been in a situation where you couldn't understand how someone felt? If yes, how did you deal with it?

Objectives:	Activities:

#1

Recognizing and interpreting non-verbal cues

Learn to recognize and interpret non-verbal cues.

- **Video modeling:** Show videos of different social interactions without sound. Ask the adolescent to observe and describe people's feelings based on body language and facial expressions.
- **Feelings game:** Play games where one person plays a role that includes specific feelings, and the other has to identify and describe them.

#2

Developing communication skills

Learn how to express their feelings and communicate clearly.

- **Mirror:** Use a mirror for the adolescent to practice facial expressions. Ask them to imitate different expressions and tell you what feeling they express.
- **Direct questions:** Practice asking direct questions. Create scenarios where the adolescent has to ask the other person how they are feeling or what they are thinking if they are unsure of the received non-verbal cues.

#3

Cultivating empathy

Enhance their ability to understand and respond to other people's feelings.

- **Conversation about the story:** Read the story with the adolescent and discuss Mary's feelings. Ask them how they think Mary feels and why.
- **Role-playing:** Pretend to be someone and ask the adolescent to respond to your feelings. For example, play a friend who is sad and ask the adolescent to show empathy and offer support.

#4

Using positive communication

Learn how to use positive body language and verbal communication.

- **Imitation of positive body language:** Show pictures or videos with examples of positive body language and ask the adolescent to imitate them.
- **Repetition exercises:** Create situations where the adolescent has to repeat what the other person said to confirm that they understood correctly. It helps improve listening and comprehension.

#5

Practicing social skills

Practice social skills through practical exercises.

- **Simulations:** Create scenarios that reflect real-life situations that the adolescent may face. Practice managing these situations with an emphasis on using nonverbal cues.
- **Group Activities:** Engage in group activities where the adolescent can practice social skills in a safe environment.

#6

Monitoring and feedback

Improve skills through monitoring and feedback.

- **Asking for feedback:** Ask the adolescent to talk to friends or family members and get feedback on their communication.
- **Recording conversations:** Record conversations and analyze them with the adolescent, identifying areas for improvement.

2 Treatment plan

Situation	Feelings	Automatic thoughts	Evidence supporting these thoughts	Evidence against these thoughts	Alternative thoughts	Behavioral response
I have difficulty understanding facial expressions that show emotions such as sadness or discomfort.	Stress, confusion, insecurity. ___ ___ ___ ___ ___	I don't understand what they feel. I'm going to react the wrong way. ___ ___ ___	I often don't understand other people's expressions. My friends seem to be surprised by my reactions. ___	I'm trying to understand the expressions better. My friends are patient and help me to improve.	I can ask my friends how they feel. My friends will explain if I don't understand. ___ ___	Use direct communication, asking my friends about their feelings. Show patience and understanding.

Identifying the situation:

Identify specific situations where they find it difficult to understand the expressions of others.

Feelings:

Write down their feelings during these situations.

Automatic thoughts:

Identify their immediate thoughts about what may hinder their communication.

Evidence supporting these thoughts:

Identify why they made these thoughts.

Evidence against these thoughts:

Think about why these thoughts may be false.

Alternative thoughts:

Develop positive and constructive thoughts to replace negative ones.

Behavioral response:

Plan specific actions for imrpoving their understanding and communication.

3

Establishing and maintaining friendships

Useful tips

Story

In a similar situation:

Start conversations: Start by saying hello to your classmates and asking simple questions like "How was your weekend?" or "How did you like your homework?"

Be part of a team: Find a club or group at school that matches your interests, whether it's sports, drama, chess, or a science group. That can provide regular opportunities to meet peers with similar hobbies.

Invite a classmate: Suggest that you go out after school. It can be something simple, like going for a walk or watching a movie together.

Offer to help: If you notice a classmate struggling with an assignment or looking for an extra sports team member, you can offer your help.

Share your interests: You can share something you are passionate about, like a favorite book, game, or hobby that can initiate conversations and build connections.

Practice listening: Show genuine interest in what others are saying by listening carefully, nodding, and asking follow-up questions to keep the conversation going.

Peter sits alone in the school cafeteria, watching peers laughing and talking in groups. During his previous efforts to fit in, he felt he couldn't find common ground with the others. Peter feels it's difficult for him to establish and maintain friendships.

- How do you think Peter feels?
- If you felt like Peter, what would you do to make friends?
- How could Peter's classmates help him feel more comfortable and encourage him to participate in their activities?

3

Objectives:	**Activities:**

#1

Initiating conversations

Learn how to start conversations with classmates.

- **Conversation card game:** Create cards with questions like "What did you do this weekend?" or "How was your day? The adolescent can use these cards to practice starting conversations.
- **Conversation role-playing:** Create scenarios where the adolescent has to start a conversation. Practice in different situations (at school, at home, with friends).

#2

Becoming a member of a group

Pursue participation in group activities.

- **Interest list:** Help the adolescent list their interests and find matching school groups or extracurricular activities. Encourage them to try one or more of these.
- **Group role-playing:** Create scenarios where the adolescent has to collaborate on a group activity (e.g., a team game or school project).

#3

Inviting a classmate

Learn how to invite classmates for activities outside of school.

- **Inviting simulation:** Create scenarios where the adolescent has to invite a classmate to an activity (e.g., play together, go to the cinema). Practice expressing their proposal and dealing with possible responses.
- **Create Invitations:** Ask the adolescent to create invitations for activities they would like to do with their friends.

#4

Offering Help

Learn how to offer help to classmates.

- **Helping role-playing game:** Create scenarios where a classmate needs help with a task or activity, and the adolescent offers it.
- **Identify opportunities for help:** List situations where the adolescent can offer help to classmates (e.g., helping with homework, preparing a presentation) and discuss how they might do so.

#5

Sharing interests

Strengthen their connection with others through shared interests.

- **Interests presentation:** Ask the adolescent to present one of their favorite hobbies or interests to a small group of friends or family.
- **Shared interests conversation:** Plan conversations where the adolescent should ask peers about their interests and share theirs.

#6

Practicing listening

Learn to listen carefully and show interest in conversations.

- **Listening game:** Play games where the adolescent has to listen to a story or conversation and answer questions to check if they have understood correctly.
- **Responding to conversations:** Have the adolescent practice asking follow-up questions to show they are interested in what others are saying.

3 Treatment plan

Situation	Feelings	Automatic thoughts	Evidence supporting these thoughts	Evidence against these thoughts	Alternative thoughts	Behavioral response
I sit alone watching my peers laughing and talking in groups. _____ _____ _____ _____ _____ _____	Stress, confusion, insecurity _____ _____ _____ _____ _____ _____ _____	I don't know what to say. I will approach my classmates the wrong way. _____ _____ _____	I often don't know how to initiate a conversation. My classmates seem to be surprised by my reactions. _____ _____	I try to make new friends. I try to approach classmates with shared interests. _____ _____ _____	I can ask my classmates if I can join them. I start a conversation about a shared interest. _____ _____ _____	Listen carefully, find a point of interest and ask a relevant question. Use active listening to show interest. _____ _____ _____

Identifying the situation:

Identify specific situations where they find it difficult to participate in the conversation.

Feelings:

Write down their feelings during these situations.

Automatic thoughts:

Identify their immediate thoughts about what may hinder their communication.

Evidence supporting these thoughts:

Identify why they made these thoughts.

Evidence against these thoughts:

Think about why these thoughts may be false.

Alternative thoughts:

Develop positive and constructive thoughts to replace negative ones.

Behavioral response:

Plan specific actions for improving their understanding and communication.

4

Conflict management

 Useful tips

In a similar situation:

During a conversation, listen without planning your response. It can help you recognize the different perspectives and emotions and show others that you respect their opinions.

Learn to recognize what you feel during a conflict— confusion, anger, sadness, or something else. That helps you better manage your state of mind and communicate it more clearly.

Be honest about your thoughts and feelings without being aggressive or passive.

When speaking, use "I" statements to express your thoughts and feelings. For example, say, "I feel confused about the situation and need a little more explanation to understand better." That reduces the likelihood of sounding judgemental and makes it easier for others to listen and accept your point of view.

If you are unsure or don't fully understand the situation, ask questions. It can help clear up your confusion and show you are engaged and interested in resolving the issue. For example, say, "Can you explain why you found that comment offensive?"

After experiencing a conflict, take some time to reflect on what happened. Write down the key points of the disagreement, how you felt, your thoughts, and how you reacted. Think about what you would do differently next time.

Story

George withdraws when confronted with a disagreement, hoping that the problem will resolve itself over time. This approach, however, often leaves his emotions suppressed, leading to resentment and a sense of isolation from those around him. He finds it difficult to express his thoughts and feelings clearly.

- Why do you think George chooses to withdraw during a disagreement?
- Can you think of different ways for George to express his feelings?
- How do you react to a disagreement?

| Objectives: | Activities: |

#1
Recognizing and expressing emotions

Learn how to recognize and express their feelings during a conflict.

- **Emotion cards:** Use cards that show different emotions (anger, sadness, frustration) and ask the adolescent to identify and relate them to situations they have experienced.
- **Emotions diary:** Ask the adolescent to keep a daily diary of their feelings and what triggered them. That can help them to identify their feelings and find ways to express them.

#2
Communicating during a conflict

Learn how to communicate effectively during an argument.

- **Role-playing:** Role-play a conflict and ask the teenager to communicate their feelings. Practice phrases like "I feel that..." and "I would like you to understand that..."
- **Direct questions:** Practice asking questions to fully understand the situation before reacting (e.g., "Can you explain why you feel this way?").

#3
Understanding the perception of others

Develop the ability to understand other people's different perspectives and intentions.

- **Discussing the story:** Discuss George's story and ask the adolescent to express how they think the other people in the story feel. Ask them how George could better understand the feelings of others.
- **Reverse role-playing:** Play games where the adolescent takes the other person's position in an argument to understand their point of view.

#4
Managing emotions after the conflict

Learn how to manage emotions after a conflict and regain calm.

- **Relaxation techniques:** Teach relaxation techniques such as deep breathing, counting to ten, or short meditation exercises that can help the adolescent calm down after a conflict.
- **Recovery journal:** Ask the adolescent to record how they felt after a conflict and what they did to calm down. Discuss what worked and what didn't.

#5
Developing strategies for effective communication

Strengthen communication skills to deal with conflict in a positive way.

- **Conflict scenarios:** Create conflict scenarios and ask the teenager to find ways to manage them. Discuss the possible consequences of each strategy and which is the most effective.
- **Conflict management cards:** Create cards with positive phrases and strategies they can use during a conflict. The adolescent can choose a card when they feel a conflict approaches.

#6
Strengthening confidence in conflict resolution

Develop self-confidence and self-esteem during conflict management.

- **Recognizing successes:** Ask the adolescent to list situations where they effectively dealt with a conflict and discuss what worked well.
- **Strong statements:** Teach the adolescent to use statements to express feelings and show confidence (e.g., "I feel angry when...").

Treatment plan

Situation	Feelings	Automatic thoughts	Evidence supporting these thoughts	Evidence against these thoughts	Alternative thoughts	Behavioral response
When faced with a disagreement, I withdraw, hoping that the problem will resolve itself over time.	Anxiety, dissatisfaction, isolation.	It's better not to say anything. If I talk, I'll make things worse.	The conflicts I have avoided sometimes resolved themselves. I haven't learned to express myself in such situations.	The disagree-ments I didn't face left feelings of dissatisfactio n. My friends want to know what I think.	I can express my thoughts and feelings in a calm way. Expressing my feelings can help resolve the disagreement.	Express my thoughts and feelings when a disagreement arises. Use active listening and calming techniques.

Identifying the situation:

Identify specific situations where they feel the need to withdraw from an argument.

Feelings:

Write down their feelings during these situations.

Automatic thoughts:

Identify their immediate thoughts about what may prevent them from dealing effectively with the disagreement.

Evidence supporting these thoughts:

Identify why they made these thoughts.

Evidence against these thoughts:

Think about why these thoughts may be false.

Alternative thoughts:

Develop positive and constructive thoughts to replace negative ones.

Behavioral response:

Plan specific actions they can take to improve expressing their feelings and dealing with disagreements.

5

Recognizing and expressing emotions

Useful tips

Story

In a similar situation:

Active listening practice: Listen carefully to what everyone says without interrupting. Nod your head or make small affirmations to show that you are engaged.

Ask clarifying questions: If you don't understand something, it's okay to ask questions to get more information or clarify someone's point of view. You can say: "I'm not sure I understand. Can you explain what you meant by that comment?"

Try to express your feelings clearly: If you feel confused or uncertain about the conversation, let others know. You could say: "Can someone help me understand what happened?"

Stay calm and neutral: Try to remain calm and avoid getting caught up in the emotions caused by the situation. It's okay to stay an observer if you don't feel comfortable getting involved.

Seek support afterwards: If you're still confused after the conversation, talk to a trusted friend or adult later to help you process the situation. After the group discussion, you could say: "Can you explain what happened earlier? I want to make sure I understand."

Anna is with her friends when they start talking about a recent incident between two of them. One was offended by a comment made by the other, and the atmosphere was highly charged. During the discussion, everyone expresses their opinions and tries to understand both sides, while Anna remains silent, unable to understand their views and feelings.

- What might be the reason Anna remained silent during the discussion?
- How do you think Anna feels?
- Have you ever been in a similar situation?

Objectives:	Activities:

#1

Recognizing emotions

Help them recognize other people's feelings.

- **Emotion cards:** Create cards with different emotions (joy, sadness, anger, fear) and ask the adolescent to identify them and describe situations in which they may have felt similarly.
- **Videos and pictures:** Play videos or show pictures of people expressing different emotions. Ask the adolescent to identify the emotions and discuss why people might feel this way.

#2

Expressing emotions

Help them express their feelings.

- **Emotions diary:** Ask the adolescent to keep a diary of their feelings and the situations that triggered them. Discuss each situation.
- **Role-playing:** Create scenarios where the adolescent has to express their feelings in different situations (e.g. ,when they are angry or sad).

#3

Using doubt to improve self-confidence

Help them develop self-confidence and emotion management skills.

- **Questioning negative thoughts:** Teach the adolescent how to question negative thoughts and feelings. For example, when feeling anxious about an argument, they may ask, "Is it really that bad? How can I deal with it?"
- **Discuss positive outcomes:** Discuss possible positive outcomes from managing their feelings and encourage them to focus on them.

#4

Encouraging expression

Encourage them to express their feelings in practical situations.

- **Planning meetings:** Create opportunities for the adolescent to discuss their feelings with friends or family. You can set up a weekly meeting to discuss issues that are on their mind.
- **Sharing experiences:** Ask the adolescent to share their experiences of managing their emotions and explain how these have helped them.

#5

Recording progress

Monitor progress in recognizing and expressing emotions.

- **Progress diary:** Ask the adolescent to record the experiences, successes, and challenges they have faced in identifying and expressing their feelings.
- **Progress assessment:** Arrange regular meetings to discuss the progress they have made and plan ways to improve further.

Situation	Feelings	Automatic thoughts	Evidence supporting these thoughts	Evidence against these thoughts	Alternative thoughts	Behavioral response
Sometimes I find it difficult to understand the feelings and views of others. _____ _____ _____ _____ _____ _____ _____ _____	Embarrass-ment, confusion. _____ _____ _____ _____ _____ _____ _____ _____	I don't know what to say. I don't understand what others feel. _____ _____ _____ _____ _____ _____	I stayed silent because I didn't know what to say and I didn't understand the feelings of others. _____ _____ _____	I have been able to understand and express my views in other situations. Understan-ding the feelings of others requires practice. _____	I can learn to better understand the feelings of others by observing their expressions. _____ _____ _____ _____ _____	Observe the expressions and body language of others to better understand their feelings. Ask questions to better understand the situation and show interest in the opinions of others.

Identifying the situation:

Identify specific situations where they feel embarrassed and find it difficult to participate in conversations due to a lack of understanding of other people's feelings.

Feelings:

Write down their feelings during these situations.

Automatic thoughts:

Understand their immediate thoughts about what may prevent them from actively participating in discussions.

Evidence supporting these thoughts:

Identify why they made these thoughts.

Evidence against these thoughts:

Think about why these thoughts may be false.

Alternative thoughts:

Develop positive and constructive thoughts to replace negative ones.

Behavioral response:

Plan specific actions they can take to improve their understanding of others' feelings and their participation in discussions.

6

Team spirit

Useful tips

In a similar situation:

Try to consciously listen to what others say without thinking about your response while they are talking. This helps you to fully understand their ideas and shows that you value their contribution.

At the beginning of the task, suggest a conversation where each member has a few minutes to share their ideas and opinions without interruption. It can create a good atmosphere of inclusiveness and respect.

When someone shares an idea, try to verbalize what they said to show that you understand. For example: "If I understand correctly, you are proposing to do X because Y..." This practice can promote a positive atmosphere.

Leave room for testing and mistakes by supporting the team. This approach can reduce the pressure of committing to an idea from the start.

Showing a willingness to incorporate different suggestions can promote collaboration and reduce conflict.

After each meeting, take some time to reflect on how well the team worked together. Think about what you did well and what you could improve. That might be something in the way you communicated, listened or contributed to the overall team morale and productivity.

Story

Peter has difficulty in working with his classmates. During a group meeting to prepare a paper, he insists on following only his ideas, ignoring the suggestions of his classmates. This attitude causes tension within the group and creates a negative atmosphere. Peter's inability to interact effectively with the group and to take into account the ideas of others leads to frustration for both himself and his classmates.

- Hw do you think Peter could improve his cooperation with the team?
- Have you ever been in a similar situation?

| **Objectives:** | **Activities:** |

#1

Understanding other people's ideas

Learn to listen to and understand the ideas of others without interrupting.

- **Active listening game:** Create a game where the teenager has to listen carefully to what others say and then repeat their ideas. It can help them focus on listening and understanding.
- **Taking notes:** During a group discussion, ask the teen to take notes on their peers' ideas without responding immediately.

#2

Participating in group tasks

Learn how to participate actively and equally in group tasks.

- **Idea circle:** At the beginning of a group project, ask each member to share their ideas for a few minutes without interruption. The adolescent should wait their turn and listen carefully to others' ideas.
- **Recognizing Ideas:** Ask the adolescent to recognize others' ideas before expressing themselves. For example, they might say, "What John said is interesting, and I would like to add that..."

#3

Strengthening cooperation

Strengthen their ability to cooperate and promote the ideas of others.

- **Collaboration games:** Play games that require cooperation, such as Lego construction or strategy board games, where the adolescent must work with others to achieve a common goal.
- **Collaboration assessment:** After each group task, arrange a discussion where team members evaluate their cooperation and exchange feedback.

#4

Managing different ideas

Learn to manage different ideas and proposals without conflict.

- **Discussing alternative options:** Create scenarios with various suggestions for a specific topic and ask the adolescent to consider how all the ideas could be integrated into a common solution.
- **Selecting the best option:** During a discussion, ask the adolescent to identify the best ideas from each member of the group and explain why they find them useful.

#5

Communicating and developing feedback skills

Improve their ability to give and receive feedback.

- **Feedback game:** Teach the adolescent how to give positive feedback using phrases such as "I liked your idea for..." Practice with role-playing games.
- **Feedback circle:** After a group task, arrange a discussion where each team member gives and receives feedback on their cooperation and performance.

#6

Monitoring and recognizing progress

Monitor progress in teamwork and recognize improvements.

- **Progress diary:** Ask the adolescent to keep a journal where they record their experiences with group work and the improvements they have noticed.
- **Progress discussion:** Arrange regular meetings to discuss their progress in group work and plan ways to improve further.

Situation	Feelings	Automatic thoughts	Evidence supporting these thoughts	Evidence against these thoughts	Alternative thoughts	Behavioral response
Sometimes in group projects I insist on following only my own ideas, ignoring the suggestions of my classmates. ___ ___ ___	Frustration, anxiety, anger. ___ ___ ___ ___ ___ ___	My ideas are the best. The others don't understand the subject as well as I do. ___ ___ ___ ___	My ideas usually work. My classmates have not always had good ideas in the past. ___ ___ ___	There are times when I have worked with others, and the results have been better. My classmates may have good ideas that I haven't thought of.	Working together can improve our work. Other people's ideas can be as good or better than mine. ___ ___ ___ ___	Listen carefully to other people's ideas and discuss with them to find the best solution. Encourage the participation of everyone in the group.

Identifying the situation:

Identify specific cases where problems arise because someone else insisted on following only their ideas.

Feelings:

Write down their feelings during these situations.

Automatic thoughts:

Understand their immediate thoughts that may hinder smooth cooperation.

Evidence supporting these thoughts:

Identify why they made these thoughts.

Evidence against these thoughts:

Think about why these thoughts may be false.

Alternative thoughts:

Develop positive and constructive thoughts to replace negative ones.

Behavioral response:

Plan specific actions to improve cooperation and acceptance of other peoples' ideas.

7

Understanding and maintaining appropriate physical boundaries

Useful tips

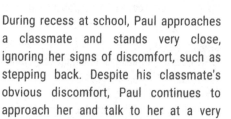

Story

In a similar situation:

Always watch the body language of others when you approach them. If they step back or move away, it may mean they need space. You can respect this by taking a step back yourself.

It's okay to ask someone if they are comfortable with the distance between you during a conversation. That not only shows respect for boundaries, but also helps you learn about different people's comfort zones.

Try practicing different scenarios at home. You can role-play with a family member, approaching them at different distances to understand when they are comfortable and when they are not.

If someone tells you or shows you that they are uncomfortable, **use it as a learning experience**. Apologize if needed and remember their boundaries next time.

Imagine that everyone has a "soap bubble" around them. Make it a rule not to "pop" someone else's bubble unless they invite you. It can help you visualize the need to maintain a distance.

After social interactions, take a minute to reflect on how it went. Think about what signs of comfort or discomfort you noticed and how you can adjust your behavior in the future based your observations.

During recess at school, Paul approaches a classmate and stands very close, ignoring her signs of discomfort, such as stepping back. Despite his classmate's obvious discomfort, Paul continues to approach her and talk to her at a very close distance, showing a lack of understanding of the concept of personal space.

- Can you describe a time when you felt uncomfortable in a similar situation? How did you feel? How did you handle it?

7

Objectives:	Activities:

#1

Observing and understanding body language

Recognize and understand signs of body language that indicate comfort or discomfort.

- **Videos and Images:** Play videos or show pictures of people in different social situations. Ask the adolescent to identify when people look cool and when they do not. Discuss what signs they noticed (e.g., facial expression, posture).
- **Real-time observation:** Do observation exercises in public places (e.g., at the park or a café) and ask the adolescent to observe people's body language and record what they observe.

#2

Asking and responding exercise

Learn to ask questions when unsure of boundaries and to respond respectfully when boundaries are violated.

- **Role-playing:** Role-play situations where the adolescent has to ask permission to do something (e.g., borrow something or sit next to someone). Teach them how to ask respectfully and accept every answer.
- **Response scenarios:** Create scenarios where personal boundaries are violated and ask the adolescent to respond respectfully (e.g., "Please, can you stand back a little?").

#3

Practicing different scenarios at home

Learn to recognize and respect the boundaries of others in different situations.

- **Family scenarios:** Role-play with family members where the adolescent must recognize and respect the boundaries of others in various situations (e.g., when someone wants some quiet or doesn't want hugs).
- **Signs of comfort and discomfort:** During family activities, ask the adolescent to observe signs of comfort and discomfort and discuss their observations.

#4

Recognizing and recalling experiences

Identify situations where they felt uncomfortable and learn how to react to them in the future.

- **Keeping journal:** Ask the adolescent to keep a journal of instances when they felt uncomfortable due to others' violating their boundaries. Discuss with them how they might react differently next time.
- **Reviewing the experiences:** Ask the adolescent to recall and describe instances when their own or others' boundaries were violated and explain how they felt in those situations.

#5

Understanding the concept of personal space

Understand the concept of personal space and the importance of maintaining it.

- **Create personal space zones:** Use colored tape to create personal space zones on the floor. Explain what each zone means (e.g., personal space, social space) and when it is appropriate to enter each zone.
- **Distance play:** Play games where the adolescent must stop when asked (e.g., when approaching someone too close) to better understand respecting the boundaries of others.

7 Treatment plan

Situation	Feelings	Automatic thoughts	Evidence supporting these thoughts	Evidence against these thoughts	Alternative thoughts	Behavioral response
Sometimes I find it difficult to understand and respect the physical boundaries of others. _____ _____ _____ _____ _____ _____ _____	Embarrass-ment, ignorance. _____ _____ _____ _____ _____ _____ _____ _____ _____	It's not a problem if I stand close to them. I don't understand why they feel uncomforta-ble. _____ _____ _____ _____ _____	I continued talking to them without noticing any reaction on their part. _____ _____ _____ _____ _____ _____ _____	My classmate took a few steps back, showing discomfort. It's important to respect other people's personal space. _____ _____ _____	It is important to observe other people's reactions. Personal space is important for everyone. _____ _____ _____ _____	Observe the reactions of others when I approach. Maintain a comfortable distance and ask if it is okay to approach. _____ _____ _____ _____

Identifying the situation:

Identify specific situations where their behavior may cause discomfort to others.

Feelings:

Write down their feelings during these situations.

Automatic thoughts:

Identify the immediate thoughts about what may hinder their understanding of the concept of personal space.

Evidence supporting these thoughts:

Identify why they made these thoughts.

Evidence against these thoughts:

Think about why these thoughts may be false.

Alternative thoughts:

Develop positive and constructive thoughts to replace negative ones.

Behavioral response:

Plan specific actions they can take to improve their understanding and respect for other people's personal space.

8

Digital communication

Useful tips

In a similar situation:

Pause to review your messages before hitting the send button. It helps avoid mistakes and gives you a chance to review your phrasing.

If you make a mistake, such as messaging the wrong person, you can acknowledge it and apologize to show maturity and responsibility.

Impulsive thoughts in a stressful situation may not always be accurate or helpful. Challenge them by asking yourself: "Is this true?" or "Is there another way to look at this?"

Practice simple stress relief techniques such as deep breathing, counting to ten, or stepping away from your mobile device for a few minutes. They can help manage your emotions before reacting.

You can talk about your worries with someone you trust. Sometimes, simply expressing your concerns openly offers reassurance and support.

Remember that every mistake is a learning opportunity. Think about what you can learn from each experience to improve how you handle similar situations in the future.

Story

Philip has difficulty using social media. Once, in an attempt to respond to a message, he accidentally sent a personal comment in the group chat, causing confusion among members. His mistake made him feel embarrassed and he avoided using the app for several days.

- How do you think Philip felt?
- If you were in Philip's shoes, what would you do to feel better?
- Have you ever been in a similar situation where you made a mistake and felt embarrassed? If yes, how did you handle it?
- What advice would you give Philip to help him overcome his embarrassment and use the app again without fear?

Objectives:	Activities:

#1

Managing messages and pausing

Learn to manage their messages and avoid impulsive responses.

- **Pausing exercises:** Practice an exercise together where the adolescent types a message, waits 5 minutes and then reads it again before sending it. Discuss if there are any points that might need to be changed or corrected.
- **Evaluating messages:** Simulate an exchange of messages where you evaluate together how appropriate their responses are before sending them.

#2

Managing mistakes

Learn to identify and correct mistakes responsibly.

- **Mistakes scenarios:** Create scenarios where the adolescent accidentally sends a message to the wrong person. Practice how they could apologize and correct their mistake.
- **Identifying mistakes exercise:** Ask the adolescent to make a list of cases where they made a mistake and explain how they corrected it. Discuss how they felt and how they can deal with it better in the future.

#3

Questioning and analyzing thoughts

Develop the ability to question stressful immediate thoughts and analyze facts.

- **Recording thoughts:** Make a list of worrisome thoughts the adolescent may have when communicating digitally. Discuss whether these thoughts are real or exaggerated and how they can challenge them.
- **Realistic thinking exercise:** Ask the adolescent to write down a stressful thought and come up with at least two alternative, more realistic thoughts.

#4

Using relaxation techniques

Learn to use relaxation techniques to manage stress caused by digital communication.

- **Breathing techniques:** Teach the adolescent simple breathing techniques, such as deep breathing or counting to ten, and practice them before sending a message.
- **Meditation and relaxation:** Guide the adolescent in a brief meditation or guided relaxation exercise when they feel stressed by digital communication.

#5

Developing communication skills

Improve communication skills through text messages.

- **Communication scenarios:** Create scenarios where the adolescent must respond to various situations through messaging. Discuss appropriate responses and the social skills needed.
- **Texting game:** Play a game where the adolescent has to respond to messages using polite and appropriate words.

#6

Monitoring progress and recognizing experiences

Monitor progress in digital communication and recognize experiences.

- **Digital communication diary:** Ask the adolescent to keep a journal where they record their experiences with digital communication, as well as their successes and challenges.
- **Recognizing experiences:** Arrange regular meetings to discuss their progress and acknowledge their improvements.

Treatment plan

Situation	Feelings	Automatic thoughts	Evidence supporting these thoughts	Evidence against these thoughts	Alternative thoughts	Behavioral response
Sometimes I send the wrong messages, causing confusion and embarrassment.	Embarrassment, awkwardness	I made a big mistake, everyone will judge me. I must not using social media again.	The chat members were confused and puzzled. I avoided using the app for days.	Most people understand that we all make mistakes. I can apologize and try to be more careful in the future.	Mistakes are human and everyone makes mistakes. I can learn from this and become better.	Apologize in the group chat, explain what happened and try to be more careful in the future.

Identifying the situation:

Identify specific occasions where they have made a mistake using social media.

Feelings:

Write down their feelings during these situations.

Automatic thoughts:

Identify the negative immediate thoughts they make after a mistake.

Evidence supporting these thoughts:

Identify why they made these thoughts.

Evidence against these thoughts:

Think about why these thoughts may be false.

Alternative thoughts:

Develop positive and constructive thoughts to replace negative ones.

Behavioral response:

Plan specific actions they can take to improve their use of social media and return to normal use.

9

First date

Useful tips

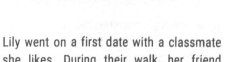

Story

In a similar situation:

Trust your feelings: It's okay to feel uncomfortable or uncertain in specific situations. Trust your instincts and acknowledge your feelings without judging them.

Communicate your boundaries: If you're still not comfortable with physical contact, it's important to communicate this to the other person. You can politely **tell them that you'd rather not hugging right now.**

Use clear language: When expressing your boundaries, use clear and direct language to ensure there is no confusion. You can say something like "I'm not ready for hugs yet, but I appreciate your understanding".

Take your time: Building comfort in a relationship takes time and it's okay to go at your own pace. No need to rush for physical affection if you're not ready.

Self-care: Take care of yourself after the experience. If you feel overwhelmed or stressed, engage in activities that help you relax and feel calm, such as listening to music, painting or going for a walk.

Seek support: If you still feel uncomfortable or unsure how to manage relationships, feel free to seek support from a trusted friend, family member or counsellor. They can offer guidance and help you feel more confident to express your needs.

Lily went on a first date with a classmate she likes. During their walk, her friend made an attempt to hug her, and she felt uncomfortable. She still doesn't feel comfortable about it.

- How do you think Lily could tell her friend that she is not yet comfortable with hugging without making him feel bad?
- Have you ever been in a similar situation? If yes, describe your experience.

Objectives:	Activities:

#1
Trusting one's feelings

Learn to trust and acknowledge their feelings without judging them.

- **Emotions diary:** Ask the adolescent to record their feelings after social interactions. Discuss these feelings with them.
- **Recognizing emotions exercise:** Create cards with different emotions and ask the adolescent to identify and associate them with situations they have experienced.

#2
Communicating one's boundaries

Learn to communicate their personal boundaries clearly and politely.

- **Role-playing:** Role-play different situations where the adolescent has to communicate their boundaries. Teach them to use phrases such as "I'm not ready for this" or "I need some time."
- **Asking for feedback:** After each role-playing exercise, have the adolescent ask for feedback from participants on how they communicated their boundaries.

#3
Using clear language

Learn to use clear and direct language to communicate feelings and boundaries.

- **Communication exercise:** Create scenarios where the adolescent must clearly communicate what they feel and need. Discuss how to use direct phrases and avoid misinterpretations.
- **Practicing in everyday life:** Encourage the adolescent to practice communicating their feelings clearly in everyday situations, such as with family or friends.

#4
Going step-by-step

Understand that relationships take time to develop and they don't need to rush.

- **Talking about relationships:** Discuss with the adolescent how healthy relationships take time and how it's normal to feel uncomfortable at first. Use examples from your own life or from movies.
- **Practicing patience:** Create scenarios where the adolescent has to develop relationships over time. Encourage them to express their concerns and take things at their own pace.

#5
Self-care and support

Learn to take care of themselves after stressful situations and to ask for support when they need it.

- **Self-care activities:** Create a list of activities that help the adolescent relax and feel better (e.g., listening to music, drawing, taking a walk). Encourage them to use them after stressful situations.
- **Talking to supportive people:** Help the adolescent identify which people in their close circle can offer support (e.g., parents, friends, teachers) and how to contact them when they need help.

#6
Seeking expert support

Understand the importance of seeking support from experts when feeling uncomfortable or anxious.

- **Talking about support:** Talk to the adolescent about the importance of mental health and how professionals can help. Explain that seeking help is a sign of strength, not weakness.
- **Learning to find support:** Give the adolescent information about where to find support (e.g., psychologists, counselors) and how to make contact.

9 Treatment plan

Situation	Feelings	Automatic thoughts	Evidence supporting these thoughts	Evidence against these thoughts	Alternative thoughts	Behavioral response
I felt uncomfortable when my friend tried to hug me. I still don't feel comfortable about that. _____ _____ _____ _____ _____ _____	Awkwardness, discomfort, embarrassment. _____ _____ _____ _____ _____ _____ _____	I don't know how to tell them that I'm not comfortable. I might disappoint them. _____ _____ _____ _____ _____	I felt uncomfortable when they tried to hug me. _____ _____ _____ _____ _____ _____ _____	It's normal not to feel ready for hugs on a first date. I can explain my feelings and set my boundaries. _____ _____ _____	It is important to be honest about my feelings. If I explain to the other person how I feel, they will understand. _____ _____ _____	Express my feelings honestly and explain that I need time to feel more comfortable. Set my boundaries in a calm and gentle way. _____ _____

Identifying the situation:

Identify specific occasions when they feel uncomfortable and awkward.

Feelings:

Write down their feelings during these situations.

Automatic thoughts:

Identify their immediate negative thoughts when facing such situations.

Evidence supporting these thoughts:

Identify why they made these thoughts.

Evidence against these thoughts:

Think about why these thoughts may be false.

Alternative thoughts:

Develop positive and constructive thoughts to replace negative ones.

Behavioral response:

Plan specific actions they can take to manage the situation and feel more comfortable.

10

Navigating in public places

Useful tips

In a similar situation:

Take deep breaths: Try taking slow, deep breaths to calm your body and mind.

Use a coping strategy: Use a coping tool, such as an anxiety ball or fidget spinner, to help refocus your attention and reduce anxiety in stressful situations.

Ask for help: Don't hesitate to ask an employee for help to find what you're looking for. It's their job to guide you.

Take a break: If you're feeling overwhelmed, step away from the situation for a few minutes. Find a quiet spot in the library where you can take a breath and regroup before continuing your search.

Make a plan: Before you visit the library, create a plan for how you will search for the book. Write down the title, author, or any other relevant details to help you stay organized and focused during your search.

Practice self-compassion: Remember that it's okay to feel frustrated or anxious when things don't go as you planned. Be kind to yourself and recognize that everyone faces challenges at times. Take a moment to reframe and approach the situation with patience and understanding.

Story

During a visit to the public library, Kevin desperately looks for a book, but he can't find it. He feels very anxious and begins to run through the aisles looking for the book, exhibiting inappropriate behavior in a public place.

- How could Kevin ask the library staff for help instead of running anxiously through the aisles?
- Have you ever been in a similar situation? If yes, describe your experience.

10

| Objectives: | Activities: |

© Upbility Publications

#1 Managing stress
Learn how to manage stress in public.

- **Breathing exercise:** Teach the adolescent to take deep breaths to calm down when anxious. Practice with them daily.
- **Use managing tools:** Give them an object, such as a fidget spinner or an exercise ball, to use when they feel anxious.

#2 Asking for help
Learn to ask for help when they need it.

- **Role-playing:** Role-play situations where the adolescent has to ask for help from an employee or other person in a public place. Practice the phrases they can use (e.g., "Can you help me find a book?").
- **Talking about the experience:** After a visit to a public place, discuss how they felt when they asked for help and what they might do differently next time.

#3 Planning and organizing
Learn to plan and organize a visit to a public place.

- **Creating a visit plan:** Ask the adolescent to create a plan for visiting a public place (e.g., a library). The plan can include writing down the title of the book he is looking for, the name of the author, and where they can find it.
- **Creating an area map:** Help them create a map of the place and mark the important spots, such as the entrance, exits, and the sections they will visit.

#4 Managing emergencies
Learn to manage emergencies calmly and confidently.

- **Emergency scenarios:** Create emergency scenarios (e.g., getting lost or not being able to find something) and practice how they will react. Discuss the steps they should take.
- **Emergency plan:** Help them create an emergency plan that they can carry with them when visiting a public place.

#5 Strengthening self-confidence
Strengthen self-confidence in public interactions.

- **Acknowledging successes:** Ask the adolescent to record their successes in public interactions and discuss how they felt and what they did well.
- **Positive reinforcement:** Encourage the adolescent to acknowledge their positive actions and remember that every experience is an opportunity for learning and improvement.

#6 Adapting to public spaces
Learn to adapt to different public spaces and situations.

- **Visiting different places:** Schedule visits to different public places (e.g., parks, museums, stores) and practice navigation and stress management strategies.
- **Discussing the experiences:** After each visit, discuss what went well, what was difficult, and how they could improve their experience next time.

10 Treatment plan

Situation	Feelings	Automatic thoughts	Evidence supporting these thoughts	Evidence against these thoughts	Alternative thoughts	Behavioral response
Sometimes I get stressed out, showing inappropriate behavior in public. ___ ___ ___ ___ ___ ___ ___	Anxiety, panic, embarrass-ment. ___ ___ ___ ___ ___ ___ ___ ___	I need to find that book now. If I don't find it, I won't be able to calm down. ___ ___ ___ ___ ___ ___ ___	I can't find the book, I panic and run all around. ___ ___ ___ ___ ___ ___ ___	The employees are there to help and I can ask them for help. I can relax and search methodically. ___ ___ ___ ___	It's normal not to always find what I'm looking for. I can ask the employees for help. ___ ___ ___ ___ ___	Ask for help from someone, calm down and look methodically. Remember that I can come back later if I don't find what I want right away.

Identifying the situation:

Identify specific situations where they feel anxiety and panic.

Feelings:

Write down their feelings during these situations.

Automatic thoughts:

Identify their immediate negative thoughts after the situation.

Evidence supporting these thoughts:

Identify why they made these thoughts.

Evidence against these thoughts:

Think about why these thoughts may be false.

Alternative thoughts:

Develop positive and constructive thoughts to replace negative ones.

Behavioral response:

Plan specific actions they can take to manage the situation and feel more comfortable.

11

Job interview

Useful tips

In a similar situation:

Practice deep breathing: Before and during interviews, take slow, deep breaths to calm your nerves and clear your mind.

Prepare your answers in advance: Write down and practice your answers to common interview questions. You will feel more prepared and confident.

Role-Play: Practice with a friend or family member by simulating the interview environment to get used to responding under pressure.

Focus on positive self-talk: Replace negative thoughts such as "I can't do this" with positive affirmations such as "I am prepared and capable."

Take your time: If you're feeling pressured, pause for a moment before responding to gather your thoughts. It's okay to take a breath and think before you speak.

Think after the interviews: After each interview, take time to think about what went well and what you can improve. Use this feedback to prepare for the next occasion.

Story

Although Jack has a good academic background and extracurricular achievements, he struggles with verbal communication under pressure, making it impossible for him to express his thoughts clearly during a part-time job interview during the summer months.

- How do you think Jack felt when he could not express his thoughts during the interview?
- Have you ever been in a similar situation? If yes, describe your experience.

11

Objectives:	Activities:

© Upbility Publications

#1

Preparing for the interview

Prepare properly for interviews, reducing stress and increasing confidence.

- **Preparing questions:** Create a list of possible questions that can be asked during the interview. Ask the adolescent to practice answering these questions.
- **Interview role-playing:** Role-play situations where the adolescent is the candidate, and you are the one taking the interview. Practice your answers and body language.

#2

Improving verbal communication

Improve verbal communication skills under pressure.

- **Breathing and relaxation exercises:** Teach the adolescent breathing and relaxation exercises to reduce stress during the interview.
- **Speaking practice:** Ask the adolescent to give a presentation on a topic they like. It will help them practice speaking in front of others.

#3

Understanding and expressing thoughts

Learn to express thoughts clearly during interviews.

- **Recognizing thoughts:** Ask the adolescent to write down their thoughts before the interview. Discuss with them how they can express them clearly.
- **Interview simulation:** Create an interview simulation and ask the adolescent to express their thoughts on various topics. Provide feedback on the clarity and structure of their responses.

#4

Strengthening of self-confidence

Strengthen self-confidence during interviews.

- **Positive self-talk:** Teach the adolescent to use positive statements about themselves before the interview (e.g., "I can do this," "I am well prepared").
- **Acknowledging successes:** Ask the adolescent to list successes and strengths. Discuss how these experiences can help them in the interview.

#5

Managing stress

Learn to manage stress during interviews.

- **Relaxation techniques:** Teach relaxation techniques such as progressive muscle relaxation or meditation to use before the interview.
- **Pausing exercise:** Practice the pause technique, where the adolescent takes a deep breath before answering a question. It gives them time to think and reduces anxiety.

#6

Using past experiences

Use past experiences to improve future performance.

- **Analyzing previous interviews:** Discuss what went well and what could be improved.
- **Record knowledge:** Help them record what they learned from each interview and how they can apply that knowledge to future interviews.

11 Treatment plan

Situation	Feelings	Automatic thoughts	Evidence supporting these thoughts	Evidence against these thoughts	Alternative thoughts	Behavioral response
I have difficulty with verbal communica-tion under pressure, which makes it difficult for me to express my thoughts clearly during an interview. _____	Anxiety, embarrass-ment. _____ _____ _____ _____ _____ _____ _____ _____	I won't be able to answer properly. I will look incompetent. _____ _____ _____ _____ _____ _____	I have difficulty expressing my thoughts when I am under pressure. _____ _____ _____ _____ _____	I have been able to communicate effectively in other situations without pressure. _____ _____ _____	I can prepare and practice interviews to make me feel more comfortable. It's normal to feel nervous, but I can manage it. _____ _____	Practice relaxation and breathing techniques to reduce stress before and during the interview. _____ _____

Identifying the situation:

Identify specific situations where they feel anxiety and shame during stressful situations.

Feelings:

Write down their feelings during these situations.

Automatic thoughts:

Identify their immediate negative thoughts when facing such situations.

Evidence supporting these thoughts:

Identify why they made these thoughts.

Evidence against these thoughts:

Think about why these thoughts may be false.

Alternative thoughts:

Develop positive and constructive thoughts to replace negative ones.

Behavioral response:

Plan specific actions they can take to manage their anxiety and shyness during such situations.

12

Social events

Useful tips

In a similar situation:

Start in small groups: Start with smaller gatherings or groups of a few friends to gradually build your comfort level with social events.

Practice relaxation techniques: Use deep breathing or relaxation exercises to calm yourself before and during social events.

Set small goals: Pursue attainable goals at each event, such as talking to one new person or staying for a certain amount of time.

Take a comfort item with you: Carry something that makes you feel safe, such as a small object or piece of jewelry.

Prepare topics to start a conversation: Think in advance about some topics or questions you can use to start conversations with others.

Reflect and adapt: After each event, take time to reflect on what went well and what you can improve for next time. Enjoy your progress and learn from each experience.

Story

Kate avoids participating in social events. Loud music and crowds cause her anxiety, making it difficult for her to initiate conversations or participate in group activities. As a result, she often declines invitations to parties, making her feel isolated and missing the opportunity to build friendships.

- How do you think Kate feels when she is at social events with loud music and lots of people?
- Have you ever been in a similar situation? If yes, describe your experience.

Objectives:	Activities:

#1

Managing stress at social events

Learn how to manage the stress caused by social events.

- **Breathing exercises:** Teach the adolescent to take deep breaths to calm down when anxious at social events. Practice daily.
- **Using coping tools:** Give them an object, such as a fidget spinner or an anti-stress ball, to use when they feel anxious.

#2

Preparing for social events

Prepare beforehand for social events to reduce stress and increase confidence.

- **Event planning:** Ask the adolescent to create a plan for the event, such as who will be present, what kind of music will be playing, and where they can find a quiet spot if they need a break.
- **Social situations role-playing:** Role-play different social situations (e.g., greeting friends, starting a conversation). Practice responses and body language.

#3

Creating a safe space

Learn to create a safe space to calm down during the event.

- **Identifying quiet places:** Upon arrival at an event, help the adolescent identify quiet places to go if they feel anxious.
- **Personal comfort zone:** Teach the adolescent to create a personal comfort zone, such as carrying a book or headphones to distract themselves.

#4

Improving social skills

Improve skills in social interactions.

- **Talking about social situations:** Talk to the adolescent about different social situations and how to handle them (e.g., how to start a conversation, how to participate in a group).
- **Communication exercise:** Create scenarios where the adolescent has to communicate with others in social situations. Discuss appropriate responses and the social skills needed.

#5

Strengthening self-confidence

Strengthen self-confidence in social events.

- **Positive self-talk:** Teach the adolescent to use positive statements before the event (e.g., "I can do this," "I am well prepared").
- **Acknowledging successes:** Ask the adolescent to list their successes at social events and discuss how they felt and what they did well.

#6

Using past experiences

Use past experiences to improve future performance.

- **Analyzing past events:** Ask the adolescent to describe their experiences at past social events. Discuss what went well and what could be improved.
- **Record knowledge:** Help them record what they learned from each event and how they can apply that knowledge to future events.

Situation	Feelings	Automatic thoughts	Evidence supporting these thoughts	Evidence against these thoughts	Alternative thoughts	Behavioral response
I have difficulty with participating in social events, resulting in declining invitations to parties and feeling isolated. ___ ___ ___	Anxiety, embarrass-ment, frustration. ___ ___ ___ ___ ___	I don't know what to say to initiate a conversation. My classmates will not include me in events in the future. ___ ___	I often decline invitations. ___ ___ ___ ___ ___	I am able to communicate in other situations. I will practice calming techniques and try to participate. ___ ___ ___	I can improve my communica-tion skills with practice. Preparation will help me feel more comfortable. ___ ___ ___	Practice calming techniques, such as deep breathing, to reduce stress. Participate in small groups as a start. ___ ___ ___

Identifying the situation:

Identify specific situations where they feel anxiety and embarrassment.

Feelings:

Write down their feelings during these situations.

Automatic thoughts:

Identify their immediate negative thoughts after the event.

Evidence supporting these thoughts:

Identify why they made these thoughts.

Evidence against these thoughts:

Think about why these thoughts may be false.

Alternative thoughts:

Develop positive and constructive thoughts to replace negative ones.

Behavioral response:

Plan specific actions they can take to manage the situation and feel more comfortable.

13

Accepting criticism

Useful tips

In a similar situation:

Take a deep breath: Before reacting to the comments, take a moment to breathe deeply and gather your thoughts.

Listen actively: Focus on listening to feedback without immediately interrupting or defending yourself. Try to understand the arguments expressed.

Ask for clarification: If you do not understand the feedback or its reasoning, politely ask the teacher for more details or examples.

Use positive self-talk: Remind yourself that feedback is meant to help you grow and improve, not to criticize you as a person.

Think before you react: Take some time after receiving feedback to reflect on it objectively. Write down the key points and think about how you can use them to improve.

Thank the person: Express your gratitude for the feedback. A simple "Thank you for your contribution" shows that you appreciate the opportunity to improve.

Story

During a project, the teacher comments on Helen's presentation, suggesting some improvements. Helen becomes upset, claiming that the criticism was unfair. Her reaction surprises the teacher and creates awkward tension in the classroom.

- How do you think Helen felt when she heard the teacher's comments?
- Have you ever been criticized and felt it was unfair? If yes, how did you react?
- What could Helen do to express her feelings without creating tension in the classroom?

13

#1
Understanding criticism
Learn to recognize that criticism can be constructive and not always negative.

- **Discussing criticism:** Explain the difference between constructive and destructive criticism. Use examples to show how constructive criticism can help development.
- **Analyzing criticism:** Ask the adolescent to think of situations where they received criticism and analyze whether it was constructive or destructive. Discuss how they could use the criticism to improve.

#2
Practicing to accept criticism
Learn to accept criticism without becoming defensive.

- **Role-playing:** Create scenarios where the teen receives criticism. Practice accepting criticism calmly and politely.
- **Recording reactions:** Ask the adolescent to record their reactions when they receive criticism and think about how they could react in a more positive way.

#3
Managing emotions
Learn to manage emotions when being criticised.

- **Relaxation techniques:** Teach relaxation techniques, such as deep breathing or counting to ten, to use when feeling tense or frustrated.
- **Emotions journal:** Ask the adolescent to keep a journal where they record their feelings when they receive criticism and how they handle it. Discuss how they can improve their emotion management.

#4
Developing communication skills
Improve communication skills when facing criticism.

- **Active listening exercise:** Teach the adolescent to listen carefully to criticism without interrupting. Ask them to repeat the criticism to make sure they understand it correctly.
- **Reaction practice:** Practice positive responses to criticism, such as "I understand what you are saying, thanks for sharing your point of view."

#5
Strengthening self-confidence
Strengthen self-confidence to deal with criticism in a positive way.

- **Recognizing strengths:** Ask the adolescent to list their strengths and accomplishments. Discuss how they can use these strengths to deal with criticism.
- **Positive self-talk:** Teach the adolescent to use positive self-statements, such as "I can learn from this criticism," "I am capable of improving."

#6
Using past experiences
Use past experiences to improve how they deal with criticism.

- **Analyzing past reactions:** Ask the adolescent to describe occasions when they have been criticized and how they reacted. Discuss what went well and what could be improved.
- **Record knowledge:** Help the adolescent record what they learned from each experience of criticism and how they can apply this knowledge to their future reactions.

13

Treatment plan

Situation	Feelings	Automatic thoughts	Evidence supporting these thoughts	Evidence against these thoughts	Alternative thoughts	Behavioral response
Sometimes I get very upset when people criticize me. _____ _____ _____ _____ _____ _____ _____ _____ _____ _____	Upset, embarrass-ment, anger. _____ _____ _____ _____ _____ _____ _____ _____ _____ _____	The teacher's criticism is unfair. He should not make such comments to me. _____ _____ _____ _____ _____ _____ _____	The teacher suggested improvements with which I do not agree. _____ _____ _____ _____ _____ _____ _____ _____	Criticism is part of the learning and improvement process. The improvements suggested can help me to become better. _____ _____ _____	Criticism can help me to improve. I can see criticism as an opportunity for growth. _____ _____ _____ _____ _____	Listen carefully to the criticism and ask for clarification if I don't understand. Evaluate the suggestions and think about how I can apply them to improve my work. _____

Identifying the situation:

Identify specific situations where they feel upset by criticism.

Feelings:

Write down their feelings during these situations.

Automatic thoughts:

Identify their immediate negative thoughts after the criticism.

Evidence supporting these thoughts:

Identify why they made these thoughts.

Evidence against these thoughts:

Think about why these thoughts may be false.

Alternative thoughts:

Develop positive and constructive thoughts to replace negative ones.

Behavioral response:

Plan specific actions they can take to manage the criticism and feel more comfortable.

14

Empathy

Useful tips

In a similar situation:

Listen actively: When someone shares their problems, concentrate on listening without interrupting. Show that you are paying attention by nodding and maintaining eye contact.

Validate feelings: Acknowledge the person's feelings by saying things like: "That sounds really harsh" or "I understand why you are upset."

Avoid comparisons: Instead of comparing their problems to others, focus on the specific situation and their feelings.

Ask open-ended questions: Encourage them to share more by asking questions like "Can you tell me more about what happened?" Or "How do you feel about it now?"

Offer support: Show that you care by offering help or just being there for them. Say things like "I'm here for you" or "What can I do to help?".

Think about your responses: After the conversations, take some time to reflect on how you responded and think of ways to be even more supportive and understanding next time.

Story

Liam is with his friends in a café, and a classmate shares that he feels very stressed about something that happened to his family. The others express support and share their own experiences to create a supportive environment, but Liam interrupts by saying that everyone faces problems and should just get through them. His response hurts his classmate, who sought compassion, and Liam is troubled.

- How do you think Liam's classmate felt when he heard his response?
- Have you ever been in a situation where someone shared their feelings with you and found it difficult to empathize with them? What did you do then?

14

Objectives:	Activities:

#1

Understanding other people's emotions

Learn to recognize and understand the feelings of others.

- **Emotion cards:** Use cards that show different emotions, ask the adolescent to identify the emotion, and associate it with a situation that might cause it.
- **Videos and pictures:** Play videos or show pictures of people in different situations and ask the adolescent to describe how these people might be feeling and why.

#2

Developing active listening skills

Learn to listen carefully to others and respond empathetically.

- **Role-playing:** Role-play where one person is sharing a problem and the other person must listen carefully and respond with words of empathy (e.g., "I understand that what you are saying is difficult. How can I help?").
- **Identifying active listening:** Ask the adolescent to observe and describe how people show that they are actively listening (e.g., by nodding their heads, asking questions).

#3

Practicing empathy

Learn to express empathy and show understanding to others.

- **Support scenarios:** Create scenarios where someone shares a problem and ask the adolescent to express empathy and support.
- **Discussing everyday situations:** Discuss everyday situations where someone might need support and how they might express empathy in those situations.

#4

Developing communication skills

Learn to communicate their empathy.

- **Open-ended questions:** Teach the adolescent to ask open-ended questions that encourage others to share their feelings (e.g., "How do you feel about this?").
- **Practicing reactions:** Practice positive reactions when someone shares a problem, such as showing understanding and support without offering immediate solutions unless asked.

#5

Strengthening self-confidence in expressing empathy

Build confidence in expressing empathy and support.

- **Acknowledging successes:** Ask the adolescent to record their successes in expressing empathy and discuss how they felt and what they did well.
- **Positive self-talk:** Teach the adolescent to use positive self-statements, such as "I can be understanding and supportive," or "I am a good listener."

#6

Past Experiences analysis

Use past experiences to improve their capacity for empathy.

- **Analyzing past situations:** Ask the adolescent to describe situations where someone shared their feelings with them and how they reacted. Discuss what went well and what could be improved.
- **Recording knowledge:** Help the adolescent record what they learned from each experience and how they can apply that knowledge to future interactions.

14 Treatment plan

Situation	Feelings	Automatic thoughts	Evidence supporting these thoughts	Evidence against these thoughts	Alternative thoughts	Behavioral response
Sometimes my words hurt my friends, but I don't do it on purpose. ___ ___ ___ ___ ___ ___ ___	Embarrass-ment, anxiety, guilt. ___ ___ ___ ___ ___ ___ ___ ___ ___	I have to say something to help. It's not that serious, he needs to get over it. ___ ___ ___ ___ ___ ___	My response hurt my classmate. I didn't know how to respond. ___ ___ ___ ___ ___ ___	My friends offered their support and understand-ing. Empathy helps people feel that they are not alone. ___ ___ ___	It is important to listen and offer support. Empathy helps to understand the feelings of others. ___ ___ ___ ___	Listen carefully and show understand-ing. Offer words of support and share my own experiences to help. ___ ___ ___

Identifying the situation:

Identify specific settings where they feel embarrassed and anxious when dealing with emotionally charged situations.

Feelings:

Write down their feelings during these situations.

Automatic thoughts:

Identify their immediate thoughts that come to mind.

Evidence supporting these thoughts:

Identify why they made these thoughts.

Evidence against these thoughts:

Think about why these thoughts may be false.

Alternative thoughts:

Develop positive and constructive thoughts to replace negative ones.

Behavioral response:

Plan specific actions they can take to manage the situation and offer support and understanding to others.

15

Phone conversations

Useful tips

In a similar situation:

Prepare notes: Before the call, note down the key points and questions you want to cover. It helps you stay focused and reduces stress.

Use clarifying questions: If you're not sure about something, ask for clarification. Phrases like "Can you repeat that?" or "What do you mean by that?" can be very helpful.

Practice active listening: Focus on the other person's words and repeat what you understand. For example: "So what you are saying is..."

Take deep breaths: If you are feeling anxious, take a few deep breaths before and during the call to calm down.

Choose a quiet environment: Make your calls in a quiet place where you can concentrate without distractions, which can help you better interpret the conversation.

Think after the calls: After each call, take some time to think about what went well and what you could improve. Use this reflection to boost your confidence for future calls.

Story

Mary has a hard time with phone conversations. She has difficulty interpreting tone of voice and non-verbal cues, resulting in frequent misunderstandings and stress during calls.

- How do you think Mary feels when she has difficulty interpreting tone of voice and non-verbal cues in phone conversations?
- Have you ever been in a situation where you had difficulty understanding what someone meant during a phone conversation? What did you do then?
- What could Mary do to reduce her anxiety and avoid misunderstandings on phone calls?

15

#1

Familiarizing with tone of voice and non-verbal cues

Learn to recognize and understand tone of voice and non-verbal cues.

- **Listening to voice samples:** Listen to recordings of different voice tones and ask the adolescent to identify the emotion being expressed (e.g., joy, sadness, anger).
- **Imitation game:** Play games where the adolescent imitates the tone of voice and expressions of others. Such games can help them become familiar with non-verbal cues.

#2

Developing listening skills

Improve active listening during phone conversations.

- **Role-playing:** Create scenarios where the adolescent has to make a phone call and practice active listening. Encourage them to repeat what they heard to make sure they understand correctly (e.g., "If I understand correctly, you say...").
- **Taking notes during calls:** Ask the adolescent to take notes during phone calls to keep track of the conversation and reduce misunderstandings.

#3

Practicing understanding and responding to feelings

Learn to understand the feelings of others and respond appropriately.

- **Emotions scenarios:** Create scenarios where someone expresses an emotion over the phone and ask the adolescent to identify the emotion and respond appropriately (e.g., "You sound upset, do you want to talk about it?").
- **Recognizing emotions in TV shows:** Watch TV shows or movies together and ask the adolescent to identify the emotions of the characters based on their tone of voice and expressions.

#4

Managing stress during phone conversations

Learn to manage the stress caused by phone conversations.

- **Relaxation techniques:** Teach the adolescent relaxation techniques, such as deep breathing or progressive muscle relaxation, to use before and during phone conversations.
- **Preparing for conversations:** Create a list of key points they want to discuss during a phone call. It will help them feel more structured and less stressed.

#5

Strengthening confidence in phone conversations

Boost confidence in phone conversations.

- **Acknowledging successes:** Ask the adolescent to record their successes on phone conversations and discuss how they felt and what they did well.
- **Positive self-talk:** Teach the adolescent to use positive self-statements before phone calls (e.g., "I can do this," "I'm good at conversations").

#6

Using technology for help

Learn to use technology to improve phone conversations.

- **Record conversations:** If possible, ask the adolescent to record phone conversations (with the other party's permission) so that they can listen to them again to improve their skills.

Situation	Feelings	Automatic thoughts	Evidence supporting these thoughts	Evidence against these thoughts	Alternative thoughts	Behavioral response
I sometimes find it difficult to interpret the tone of voice and non-verbal cues, resulting in frequent misunderstandings and stress during calls. _____	Anxiety, embarrassment, frustration. _____ _____ _____ _____ _____ _____ _____ _____	I can't understand what others are thinking. I'll say something wrong. _____ _____ _____ _____ _____ _____	I have difficulty interpreting the tone of voice and the clues. _____ _____ _____ _____ _____	Phone conversations are more difficult because there are no visual cues. I can ask for clarification if I don't understand something. _____	Practice will help me feel more comfortable. _____ _____ _____ _____ _____ _____ _____ _____	Practice phone conversations with friends or family. Ask for clarification when I don't understand something. Use calming techniques before and during calls.

Identifying the situation:

Identify specific situations where they feel anxious and uncomfortable during phone conversations.

Feelings:

Write down their feelings during these situations.

Automatic thoughts:

Identify their immediate negative thoughts during calls.

Evidence supporting these thoughts:

Identify why they made these thoughts.

Evidence against these thoughts:

Think about why these thoughts may be false.

Alternative thoughts:

Develop positive and constructive thoughts to replace negative ones.

Behavioral response:

Plan specific actions they can take to improve their experience of phone conversations.

16

Asking for help

Useful tips

In a similar situation:

Practice deep breathing: Before and during games, take slow, deep breaths to calm down and clear your mind.

Set realistic goals: Focus on setting attainable goals based on effort and improvement, and don't strive for perfection in every game.

Use positive self-talk: Replace negative thoughts with positive affirmations, such as "I'm doing my best" or "It's okay to make mistakes."

Communicate with your coach: Feel free to share feelings of pressure and anxiety with your coach. They are there to support you.

Reflect on your performance: After each game, take time to reflect on what went well and what you can improve on, focusing on the positive aspects of your performance.

Take care of yourself: Make sure you get plenty of rest, eat well, and take care of your mental health. Balance in life helps to better manage stress and anxiety.

Story

Samuel is very good at football. But he feels a lot of pressure to perform perfectly in every game. His anxiety is unbearable, but he doesn't know how to ask for help. One night, his coach noticed his tension and asked if something was wrong. Samuel had a hard time managing it.

- What do you think Samuel could have said to his coach?
- Have you ever been in a similar position?
- How do you think the coach could help Samuel manage his anxiety?
- What would you advise him to do?

16

#1

Identifying when and how to ask for help

Learn when and how to ask for help in different situations.

- **Role-playing:** Create scenarios where the adolescent needs to ask for help. Role-play with the adolescent as the person asking for help and you as the person providing help. Practice the language they can use.
- **Recording situations:** Ask the adolescent to write down situations in which they may need help (e.g., at school, in their sports team, at home) and think about how they might ask for help in each situation.

#2

Developing confidence to seek help

Build confidence in expressing their needs.

- **Discussing possibilities:** Discuss their capabilities and accomplishments. Emphasize that asking for help is a skill that shows maturity and self-awareness.
- **Positive feedback:** When the adolescent asks for help, give positive feedback and praise them for their initiative.

#3

Managing stress

Learn to manage the stress caused by having to ask for help.

- **Relaxation techniques:** Teach the adolescent relaxation techniques, such as deep breathing or progressive muscle relaxation, to use before asking for help.
- **Journal:** Ask the adolescent to record the times they felt anxiety and how they managed it.

#4

Cooperating with others

Learn to cooperate and ask for help from others.

- **Group activities:** Engage in group activities where the adolescent needs to work with others and ask for help. Practice using phrases such as "Can you help me with this?"
- **Talk about teamwork:** Discuss the importance of teamwork and how asking for help improves cooperation skills.

#5

Preparing for possible situations

Prepare for possible situations where they may need to ask for help.

- **Situation planning:** Ask the adolescent to plan how they will ask for help in various situations they may encounter. Discuss possible responses and how they will manage them.
- **Contact list:** Help the adolescent create a list of contacts (e.g., teachers, coaches, friends) to whom they can turn for help. Discuss when and how they might be contacted.

#6

Analyzing past experiences

Use past experiences to improve skills.

- **Past situations analysis:** Ask the adolescent to describe situations where they have asked or should have asked for help. Discuss what went well and what could be improved.
- **Record knowledge:** Help the adolescent record what they learned from each experience and how they can apply that knowledge to future interactions.

16 Treatment plan

Situation	Feelings	Automatic thoughts	Evidence supporting these thoughts	Evidence against these thoughts	Alternative thoughts	Behavioral response
Sometimes I don't know how to ask for help when I really need it. ___ ___ ___ ___ ___ ___ ___ ___	Stress, pressure, embarrass-ment. ___ ___ ___ ___ ___ ___ ___ ___ ___	I have to be perfect in every game. If I don't perform well, I'll let people down. ___ ___ ___ ___ ___ ___	I feel a lot of pressure and anxiety before every game. ___ ___ ___ ___ ___ ___ ___	Everyone makes mistakes and perfection is not a realistic goal. Effort and improvement are more important. ___ ___	Perfection is not necessary, continuous effort is important. I can talk to the coach about my anxiety. ___ ___ ___	Explain to the coach how I feel and ask for support and guidance. Practice calming techniques and focus on improving and enjoying the game. ___

Identifying the situation:

Identify specific situations where they feel stress and pressure to perform perfectly.

Feelings:

Write down their feelings during these situations.

Automatic thoughts:

Identify their immediate negative thoughts during games.

Evidence supporting these thoughts:

Identify why they made these thoughts.

Evidence against these thoughts:

Think about why these thoughts may be false.

Alternative thoughts:

Develop positive and constructive thoughts to replace negative ones.

Behavioral response:

Plan specific actions they can take to manage stress and feel more comfortable asking for help.

17

Responding to bullying in a positive way

© Upbility Publications

Useful tips

In a similar situation:

Be supportive: Offer your classmate your friendship and support. Let them know that they are not alone and that you care about their well-being.

Speak up: If you feel safe, stand up to bullies by calmly telling them their behavior is unacceptable. Sometimes, saying "That's not right" can go a long way.

Encourage participation: Invite your classmate to participate in group activities and class discussions to help them feel included and valued despite the negative behavior of others.

Report bullying: Report the incident to a teacher, counselor, or other trusted adult. They can take appropriate action to address the situation.

Be a role model: Show kindness and respect in your interactions with everyone. Your positive behavior can influence others to do the same.

Offer to listen: Sometimes, being there to listen to your classmate can provide much-needed support and comfort. Let them express their feelings without judging them.

Story

Emma notices that one of her classmates, Henry, is targeted by a group of students. The group often teases Henry about his hobbies and outfits, making mean comments and laughing. The situation becomes increasingly unpleasant and affects Henry's participation in class.

- How do you think Henry feels when he is teased? How does this affect his participation in class?
- If you were in Emma's shoes, what would you do to help Henry and address the problem?
- How could Emma talk to the kids who tease Henry to make them understand how it affects him?

17

#1

Understanding bullying and its consequences

Learn to recognize what bullying is and how it affects others.

- **Presentations and open discussions:** Talk about what bullying is and how it affects individuals. Encourage discussion and questions from students.
- **Examples and stories:** Use real-life examples and stories to show the consequences of bullying.

#2

Developing empathy skills

Develop the ability to put themselves in the other person's shoes and understand their feelings.

- **Role-play activities:** Create scenarios where adolescents play the roles of victim, bully and observer. Discuss their feelings and reactions.
- **Emotion discussions:** Discuss the emotions caused by bullying and how they can recognize them in others.

#3

Strengthening confidence and reaction skills

Build self-confidence and learn how to react positively to bullying.

- **Response tips:** Teach adolescents how to respond positively and confidently to bullying. Use examples and practical exercises.
- **Reaction scenarios:** Create scenarios where they have to react to incidents of bullying. Discuss their reactions and improve their skills.

#4

Fostering positive social behaviors

Learn how to support peers and promote positive social behaviors.

- **Support groups:** Create support groups where adolescents can discuss their problems and find solutions together.
- **Collaborative activities:** Promote activities that encourage cooperation and mutual support among them.
- **Reward positive behaviors:** Reward and recognize their positive behaviors and efforts to support their peers.

17

Treatment plan

Situation	Feelings	Automatic thoughts	Evidence supporting these thoughts	Evidence against these thoughts	Alternative thoughts	Behavioral response
I am an observer to an incident of bullying.	Sadness, anger, anxiety fear.	I have to do something to help. If I talk, they might target me too.	Henry seems very sad and isolated.	The support of a friend can make a big difference. Adults at school are there to help and ensure a safe environment for everyone.	I can talk to a teacher about the situation. I can show Henry that he has friends who support him.	Talk to a teacher or counselor about Henry's situation. Try to be friendly and supportive to him, showing that he is not alone.

Identifying the situation:

Identify specific situations where someone is being targeted and teased.

Feelings:

Write down their feelings during these situations.

Automatic thoughts:

Identify their immediate thoughts about the situation.

Evidence supporting these thoughts:

Identify why they made these thoughts.

Evidence against these thoughts:

Think about why these thoughts may be false.

Alternative thoughts:

Develop positive and constructive thoughts to replace negative ones.

Behavioral response:

Plan specific actions they can take to support their classmate and manage the situation.

18

Public speech

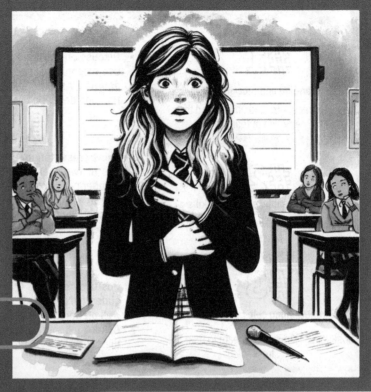

Useful tips

In a similar situation:

Practice deep breathing: Before and during your presentation, take slow, deep breaths to calm yourself.

Focus on friendly faces: Look for supportive faces in the audience. Focusing on these positive cues can help reduce anxiety and boost your confidence.

Prepare thoroughly: Practice your presentation several times to familiarize yourself with the subject. The more prepared you are, the more confident you will feel.

Use positive self-talk: Replace negative thoughts with positive affirmations. Tell yourself, "I am prepared," or "I can do this."

Start strong: Start your presentation with a strong, clear statement or an interesting fact to attract attention and build your confidence.

Acknowledge your success: After your presentation, take a moment to appreciate your achievement. Reflect on the positive comments and the applause, and acknowledge that you faced your fear and succeeded.

Story

Jenny's heart is pounding as she stands in front of the classroom, her classmates watching her presentation. Public speaking makes her uncomfortable, but she takes a deep breath and begins to speak. Her voice is shaky at first, but she focuses on her teacher's encouraging smile. In the end, Jenny feels better as her classmates applaud her, knowing she faced her fear and succeeded.

- How do you think Jenny felt as she stood in front of the class ready to make her presentation?
- What do you think helped Jenny overcome her anxiety and complete her presentation successfully?
- Have you ever been in a similar situation where you felt nervous about speaking in front of an audience? How did you deal with it and what did you do to feel better?

18

#1

Understanding and recognizing fear

Learn to recognize and understand the emotion of fear.

- **Discussion on fear:** Discuss what fear is and how it feels. Use examples from everyday life.
- **Journal:** Ask the adolescent to record the times they feel fear and describe the situation that caused it.

#2

Developing public speaking skills

Improve public speaking skills and reduce anxiety.

- **Short presentations:** Practice short presentations in front of one or two friends or family members. Slowly increase the number of people.
- **Use of visual aids:** Teach the adolescent how to use visual aids, such as slides or note cards, to help them with their presentation.

#3

Strengthening self-confidence

Boost self-confidence and learn to manage stress.

- **Positive self-talk:** Teach the adolescent to use positive self-statements before a presentation (e.g., "I can do this," "I am well prepared").
- **Acknowledging successes:** Ask the adolescent to record their successes in presentations and discuss how they felt.

#4

Relaxation techniques

Learn to use relaxation techniques to reduce stress before and during a public speech.

- **Breathing exercises:** Teach the adolescent how to take deep breaths to calm down before the presentation. Practice with them daily.
- **Progressive muscle relaxation:** Teach the adolescent how to relax each muscle group of their body one by one, starting with the legs and working up to the head.

#5

Preparing for the presentation

Prepare properly for the presentation to reduce anxiety and enhance confidence.

- **Presentation plan:** Help the adolescent create a plan for their presentation, including the key points they want to cover and the slides or visual aids they will use.
- **Presentation rehearsal:** Ask the adolescent to rehearse their presentation in front of a mirror or in front of family members or friends. Encourage them to repeat the presentation several times until they feel comfortable.

#6

Dealing with criticism

Learn to accept criticism in a positive way and use feedback to improve.

- **Talk about criticism:** Explain to the adolescent the difference between constructive and negative criticism. Discuss how constructive criticism can help their development.
- **Responding to criticism:** Teach the adolescent how to respond to criticism with kindness and positivity. Practice scenarios where they receive criticism and ask them to respond with phrases such as "Thank you, I'll take that into consideration."

18

Treatment plan

Situation	Feelings	Automatic thoughts	Evidence supporting these thoughts	Evidence against these thoughts	Alternative thoughts	Behavioral response
I find it very difficult to talk in front of people. _____ _____ _____ _____ _____ _____ _____ _____	Anxiety, embarrass-ment, fear, relief, pride. _____ _____ _____ _____ _____ _____ _____	I'm not gonna make it. I will make a mistake and everyone will laugh. _____ _____ _____ _____ _____ _____	My voice was shaking at first. _____ _____ _____ _____ _____ _____ _____	My teacher smiled encouragingly. My classmates applauded at the end of the presentation. _____ _____ _____ _____ _____	I can do it even if I'm stressed. The support of others can help me feel better. _____ _____ _____ _____ _____ _____	Remember the positive experiences and focus on the encouraging signs. Prepare well and practice calming techniques before each presentation.

Identifying the situation:

Identify specific situations where they feel anxious and embarrassed during public speaking.

Feelings:

Write down their feelings during these situations.

Automatic thoughts:

Identify their immediate negative thoughts before and during the speech.

Evidence supporting these thoughts:

Identify why they made these thoughts.

Evidence against these thoughts:

Think about why these thoughts may be false.

Alternative thoughts:

Develop positive and constructive thoughts to replace negative ones.

Behavioral response:

Plan specific actions they can take to improve their self-confidence and manage their anxiety.

19

Time management

Useful tips

In a similar situation:

Prioritize tasks: Make a list of your tasks and prioritize them by importance and deadlines.

Create a schedule: Schedule your day, setting aside specific time slots for study and social activities. For example, study from 4 p.m. to 6 p.m. and then go to the party from 7 p.m. onward.

Set clear goals: Set specific goals for your reading.

Stay focused: Minimize distractions while studying to make the most of your time. Turn off your phone or use social media blocking apps to help you stay focused.

Contact teachers: If you're struggling to balance your commitments, talk to your teachers for advice.

Reward yourself: Use social activities as a reward for completing your study goals. For example, after studying for two hours, enjoy a guilt-free party knowing that you prepared for your test.

Story

Linda is excited about her friend's party but worried about the upcoming history test. Balancing her social life with her schoolwork always seems difficult. After discussing it with her teacher, she decides to study for two hours before the party. That way, she can enjoy the time with her friends and feel prepared for the test. Linda realizes that with a little planning she can manage her responsibilities and have fun as well.

- How do you think Linda felt when she realized she could combine studying for the history test and her friend's party?
- What do you think Linda learned from this experience about managing her time?
- Have you ever been in a similar situation where you had to find a balance between schoolwork and social life? What did you do?

19

#1

Identifying priorities

Learn to identify and set clear priorities.

- **Priority list:** Ask the adolescent to write down all their responsibilities (e.g., schoolwork, social activities, hobbies) and prioritize them based on importance and urgency.
- **Discussing priorities:** Discuss why they chose this prioritization and how they can manage their time more effectively.

#2

Creating a timetable

Learn to create and follow a timetable to manage time effectively.

- **Weekly schedule:** Help the adolescent create a weekly schedule that includes time for study, social activities, and relaxation. Use a calendar or digital app to help them get organized.
- **Schedule evaluation:** After a week, discuss how the schedule went. What worked well, and what needs improvement?

#3

Using time management techniques

Learn various time management techniques that can help them be more efficient.

- **Pomodoro Technique:** Teach the adolescent the Pomodoro technique, where they work for 25 minutes and then take a 5-minute break. After four cycles, they take a longer break.
- **Time analysis:** Ask the adolescent to record how they spend their time for a day. Analyze with them how they could use their time more effectively.

#4

Balancing school and social life

Learn to maintain a balance between school obligations and social life.

- **Discussing about balance:** Discuss the importance of balance between school and social life. Explain how this balance can improve mental and physical health.
- **Balance scenarios:** Create scenarios where the adolescent must find ways to balance school responsibilities and social activities. Ask them to suggest solutions and discuss with them possible ways of managing them.

Situation	Feelings	Automatic thoughts	Evidence supporting these thoughts	Evidence against these thoughts	Alternative thoughts	Behavioral response
Sometimes I find it difficult to manage my time and as a result I miss important events. ___ ___ ___ ___ ___ ___ ___	Worry, anxiety. ___ ___ ___ ___ ___ ___	I will not have enough time to study and have fun. If I go to the party, I will fail the test. ___ ___ ___ ___	It's difficult to balance my commitments ___ ___ ___ ___ ___	With the right planning, I can have time for studying and having fun. I've managed to balance the two in the past. ___ ___ ___	I can plan my time to read and have fun. Fun and relaxation are important for effective learning. ___ ___ ___ ___	Schedule two hours of study before the party. Enjoy time with my friends. Continue to use scheduling to manage my responsibili- ties. ___

Identifying the situation:

Identify specific situations where they feel stressed about balancing school and social responsibilities.

Feelings:

Write down their feelings during these situations.

Automatic thoughts:

Identify their immediate negative thoughts when facing such situations.

Evidence supporting these thoughts:

Identify why they made these thoughts.

Evidence against these thoughts:

Think about why these thoughts may be false.

Alternative thoughts:

Develop positive and constructive thoughts to replace negative ones.

Behavioral response:

Plan specific actions they can take to improve their ability to manage time and stress.

20

Figurative language

that was a joke! Didn't you get it?

Useful tips

In a similar situation:

Learn common phrases: Familiarize yourself with common sarcastic phrases and their meanings. For example, "You're a real Einstein!" often means that someone made a simple mistake, not that they are actually a genius.

Pay attention to tone and context: Pay attention to the tone of voice and the context in which something is said. Sarcasm is often accompanied by a certain tone and is used in situations where the literal meaning doesn't fit.

Ask for clarification: If you're not sure if a comment is sarcastic, it's okay to ask. For example, you can say, "Are you kidding?" or "Did you mean that literally?" That can help clarify the intent.

Stay calm and think: Take a minute to think before responding. If something seems confusing, keeping calm can help you interpret it better. For example, pause and think: "Is this something my friend would normally say as a joke?"

Learn from experience: Reflect on past experiences in which sarcasm was used. Understanding how it was used in the past can help you recognize it in the future.

Communicate your feelings: If sarcastic comments bother you, tell your friends. For example, you can say, "Sometimes I have a hard time telling when you're joking. Can you be more clear?" That helps create a more understanding and supportive environment.

Story

During class, Mike makes a mistake in math, and his friend says: "Wow, you're a real Einstein!" Mike feels confused and replies, "But I'm not a scientist." His friends laugh, realizing that Mike took the comment literally. Later, his friend explained it was just a sarcastic joke and not a literal statement.

- How do you think Mike felt when he heard the comment and didn't realize it was sarcastic?
- Why do you think Mike's friends laughed when he responded literally to the comment?
- Have you ever been in a similar situation where you didn't understand a funny or sarcastic comment? How did you handle it and what did you do to understand the other person's intent?

Objectives:	Activities:

#1

Understanding sarcasm

Learn to recognize and understand sarcasm.

- **Examples of sarcasm:** Give examples of sarcastic comments and discuss the difference between a literal and a sarcastic statement. Ask the adolescent to identify sarcasm in the examples.
- **Role-playing:** Role-play by using sarcastic comments and asking the adolescent to identify which comments are sarcastic and which are not.

#2

Recognizing emotions

Learn to recognize the emotions that sarcastic comments can cause.

- **Discussion of feelings:** Discuss how someone might feel when they hear a sarcastic comment. Ask the adolescent to describe the emotions that Mike felt in the story.
- **Recognizing emotions:** Use pictures of people expressing different emotions and ask the adolescent to identify and associate them with situations where they hear sarcastic comments.

#3

Dealing with sarcasm and jokes

Learn to deal with sarcasm and jokes in a positive way.

- **Responding to sarcasm:** Teach the adolescent how to respond to sarcastic comments without feeling uncomfortable. Practice responses such as "I got the joke" or "Oh, that was sarcastic!"
- **Managing jokes:** Play games where the adolescent has to create their own jokes or sarcastic comments and share them with you. It can help them become familiar with the process of creating and understanding jokes.

#4

Practicing social interaction

Improve social interaction skills.

- **Group activities:** Participate in group activities where the adolescent can interact with others and practice understanding sarcasm and jokes.
- **Discussion about communication:** Discuss the importance of good communication and how different modes of expression, such as sarcasm, can affect understanding and interacting.

#5

Reviewing and reflecting

Reflect on experiences and identify what they have learned about understanding sarcasm and jokes.

- **Journal of interactions:** Ask the adolescent to keep a journal in which they record the times they heard sarcastic comments or jokes and how they reacted. Discuss what they learned from these experiences.
- **Improvement plan:** Help the adolescent create a plan for how they can improve their skills in understanding and responding to sarcasm and jokes. Discuss specific actions they will take.

Situation	Feelings	Automatic thoughts	Evidence supporting these thoughts	Evidence against these thoughts	Alternative thoughts	Behavioral response
Sometimes I don't understand my classmates' jokes. I confuse literal and figurative language. ___ ___ ___ ___	Confusion, embarrassment. ___ ___ ___ ___ ___ ___ ___	I don't understand what that means. I have to answer literally. ___ ___ ___ ___ ___	I answered literally and my friends laughed. ___ ___ ___ ___ ___	My friends explained that it was a sarcastic joke. People often use sarcasm for humor. ___ ___ ___	Sarcasm is a form of humor that should not be taken literally. I can ask for clarification when I don't understand something. ___	Observe body language and tone of voice to understand sarcasm. Ask for clarification when I don't know if something is a joke or not. ___ ___

Identifying the situation:

Identify specific instances where they feel confused by sarcastic comments or non-literal statements.

Feelings:

Write down their feelings during these situations.

Automatic thoughts:

Identify their immediate thoughts when facing such situations.

Evidence supporting these thoughts:

Identify why they made these thoughts.

Evidence against these thoughts:

Think about why these thoughts may be false.

Alternative thoughts:

Develop positive and constructive thoughts to replace negative ones.

Behavioral response:

Plan specific actions they can take to improve their understanding and reaction to sarcastic comments.

21

Resisting negative influences

In a similar situation:

Learn your values: Identify and stick to your values and what you believe is right.

Practice saying no: Develop and practice ways to say no with confidence. For example, you can say: "No, thank you. I need to stay in class" or "I don't want to miss this class."

Suggest alternatives: Offer other options that align with your values. For example, "Let's get together after school" or "How about we go to the park this weekend?"

Ask for support from people you trust: Talk to someone you trust, such as an older sibling, teacher or counselor, for advice and support. They can help strengthen your decision and encourage you.

Consider the consequences: Think about the possible consequences of your actions before you make a decision. For example, think about how skipping class could affect your grades and future opportunities.

Choose your friends wisely: Choose friends who respect your choices and share similar values. Being with supportive friends can make it easier to resist peer pressure.

Story

Thomas feels uncomfortable as his friends urge him to leave class and go to the park with them. Wanting to fit in, he reluctantly agrees, even though he knows it's wrong. As time passes, Thomas feels more and more guilty and worried about the missed class. Later, he confides in his sister, who encourages him to make his own choices and stand up for what he believes is right. Thomas realizes that he must find the courage to resist negative influences in the future.

- How do you think Thomas felt?
- What do you think Thomas learned from his experience when he felt guilty and worried about the missed class?
- Have you ever been in a similar situation where you felt pressure from your friends to do something you knew was wrong? How did you handle it, and what did you do to defend what you thought was right?

21

#1

Understanding peer pressure

Learn to recognize and understand peer pressure.

- **Conversation about peer pressure:** Discuss what peer pressure is and how they can recognize it. Use examples from everyday life.
- **Recording situations:** Ask the adolescent to record situations where they felt peer pressure and describe how they reacted.

#2

Developing pressure resistance skills

Learn to resist peer pressure and stand up for their values.

- **Role-playing:** Create scenarios where the adolescent is under peer pressure to do something they know is wrong. Role-play with the adolescent as the person resisting the pressure and you as the peers. Practice the phrases they may use.
- **Alternatives analysis:** Discuss alternatives that the adolescent might make when feeling peer pressure. How can they say "no" politely but firmly?

#3

Cultivating self-confidence

Build self-confidence and learn to make decisions that reflect their values.

- **Recognizing potential:** Discuss their potential and accomplishments. Emphasize the importance of self-awareness and self-confidence.
- **Positive self-talk:** Teach the adolescent to use positive self-statements when feeling peer pressure (e.g., "I can make my own choices," "I am capable of saying no").

#4

Recognizing and managing emotions

Learn to recognise emotions and manage them effectively.

- **Emotions journal:** Ask the adolescent to keep a journal recording their feelings when they experience peer pressure. Discuss what they have learned from these experiences.
- **Relaxation techniques:** Teach the adolescent relaxation techniques, such as deep breathing or progressive muscle relaxation, to use when feeling stress or pressure.

#5

Support from family and friends

Learn to ask for and receive support from family and friends.

- **Talk about support:** Explain to the adolescent that it is normal to ask for support when they need it. Discuss which people in their life can offer support (e.g., family, friends, teachers).
- **Support seeking exercise:** Create scenarios where the adolescent needs to ask for support from someone. Practice with them on the phrases they can use (e.g., "Can you help me make a decision?").

Treatment plan

Situation	Feelings	Automatic thoughts	Evidence supporting these thoughts	Evidence against these thoughts	Alternative thoughts	Behavioral response
I feel uncomfortable when my friends urge me to do things I don't want to do and I agree just to fit in.	Discomfort, guilt, anxiety.	If I don't go with them, they'll reject me. I can't say no.	My friends urged me to leave the class and I felt uncomfortable saying no.	My sister encouraged me to make my own choices and stand up for what I believe is right.	I can make my own choices and trust what I think is right. It's okay to say no when something doesn't feel right.	Practice saying no in situations where I feel pressure to do something I don't want to do. Remembering that it is important to do what I think is right and to stand up for my values.

Identifying the situation:

Identify specific situations where they feel pressure from their friends to do something they don't want to do.

Feelings:

Write down their feelings during these situations.

Automatic thoughts:

Identify their immediate thoughts when facing such situations.

Evidence supporting these thoughts:

Identify why they made these thoughts.

Evidence against these thoughts:

Think about why these thoughts may be false.

Alternative thoughts:

Develop positive and constructive thoughts to replace negative ones.

Behavioral response:

Plan specific actions they can take to improve their self-confidence and better manage pressure from their friends.

22

Participating in group discussions

Useful tips

In a similar situation:

Prepare beforehand: Read the topic before class and note the main points you might want to share. Having notes can help you feel more confident.

Practice speaking at home: Rehearse your thoughts out loud at home or with a family member. This practice can make it easier to express your ideas in class.

Start small: Start by contributing small comments or questions during class discussions. Gradually, move on to sharing more detailed thoughts.

Use deep breathing techniques: If you feel nervous, take a few deep breaths to calm yourself before speaking. This can help you clear your mind and reduce anxiety.

Focus on a friendly person: When speaking, look at a friendly or supportive classmate or the teacher. This can make you feel more comfortable.

Acknowledge your efforts: After you speak, even if it was only a few words, acknowledge that you tried. Gradually, you will become more confident.

Story

In history class, Emily quietly listens to her classmates discussing a topic. She has ideas to share but feels too nervous to speak. When the teacher calls her name, Emily's mind goes blank, and she mumbles a few words before falling silent. She feels very sad that she didn't have the courage to talk in front of her classmates about things she knew.

- How do you think Emily felt when she wanted to share her ideas but felt nervous speaking in front of the class?
- What could help Emily feel more comfortable and gain the courage to speak in front of her classmates?
- Have you ever been in a similar situation where you knew the answer or had ideas to share but felt nervous to speak up? What did you do to overcome that anxiety?

Objectives:	Activities:

#1

Recognizing and managing anxiety

Learn to recognize and manage the anxiety caused by the need to speak in front of an audience.

- **Stress journal:** Ask the adolescent to keep a journal where they record the times they feel anxious when they have to speak in front of the class. Discuss what they learned from these experiences.
- **Relaxation techniques:** Teach the adolescent relaxation techniques, such as deep breathing or progressive muscle relaxation, to use before speaking in front of the class.

#2

Developing confidence in public speaking

Develop confidence and skills to speak in front of their peers.

- **Small presentations:** Start with small presentations in front of one or two friends or family members. Slowly increase the number of people.
- **Preparing presentations:** Help the adolescent prepare their presentations by creating a plan for the key points they want to cover. Encourage them to use visual aids.

#3

Encouragement and positive self-talk

Boost self-confidence through positive self-talk and encouragement.

- **Positive affirmations:** Teach the adolescent to use positive affirmations about themselves before speaking in front of the class (e.g., "I can do this," "I am well prepared").
- **Encouraging conversation:** Discuss with the adolescent their potential and accomplishments. Emphasize the importance of self-awareness and self-confidence.

#4

Practicing social interaction

Improve social interaction skills and become more comfortable speaking in front of others.

- **Group Activities:** Engage in group activities where the adolescent can interact with others and practice speaking in front of an audience.
- **Talk about communication:** Discuss the importance of good communication and how it can improve social interactions.

Treatment plan

Situation	Feelings	Automatic thoughts	Evidence supporting these thoughts	Evidence against these thoughts	Alternative thoughts	Behavioral response
I don't have the courage to talk in front of my classmates about things I know. _____ _____ _____ _____ _____ _____ _____	Stress, sadness. _____ _____ _____ _____	I will make a mistake and make a fool of myself. The others are smarter than me. _____ _____ _____	The times when I found it difficult to express myself in public. _____ _____ _____ _____	My classmates make mistakes and no one judges them. The teacher encouraged me to speak up. _____ _____ _____	It's okay to make mistakes. Every time I speak, I learn and improve. I have important ideas to share. _____ _____ _____	Prepare before the discussions. Start talking to smaller groups and gradually increase my audience. Practice presenting my thoughts in front of a mirror or with a friend.

Identifying the situation:

Identify specific instances where they feel pressure from public exposure.

Feelings:

Write down their feelings during these situations.

Automatic thoughts:

Identify their immediate thoughts when facing such situations.

Evidence supporting these thoughts:

Identify why they made these thoughts.

Evidence against these thoughts:

Think about why these thoughts may be false.

Alternative thoughts:

Develop positive and constructive thoughts to replace negative ones.

Behavioral response:

Plan specific actions they can take to improve their confidence and gain courage for public exposure.

23

Stress management in social events

Useful tips

In a similar situation:

Concentrate on your breath: Take slow, deep breaths to calm your body and mind. For example, inhale for four seconds, hold for four and exhale for four.

Find a quiet corner: If the noise and crowds are overwhelming, retreat to a quieter corner. Sit there until you feel calmer.

Contact someone you trust: Let a friend or family member know how you are feeling. They can support you and help you feel more comfortable.

Focus on an object: Hold a small object, such as a key or a coin. This can help distract you from stress.

Use positive thoughts: Remind yourself that it's okay to feel stressed and that you have the skills to deal with it. For example, think "I can get through this, I'll be fine."

Take small steps: Instead of withdrawing completely, try to get back into the party by taking small steps. Start by talking to one person before rejoining the group.

Story

At a birthday party full of people, Charles feels his chest tight and his hands shaking. The noise and the crowd overwhelm him, making it difficult to remain calm. He retreats to a quiet corner and takes deep breaths but still finds it hard to relax.

- Have you ever felt such intense anxiety or panic as Charles did in a crowded place?
- How would you describe your feelings if you were in Charles' shoes at a birthday party?
- Have you found a way to help you relax when you feel overwhelmed by the crowd and noise?

#1

Recognizing and understanding anxiety

Learn to recognize and understand the signs of anxiety and panic.

- **Talk about anxiety:** Discuss what anxiety is and how it can affect the body and mind. Use examples and personal experiences.
- **Journal:** Ask the adolescent to keep a journal where they record when they feel anxious or panicky and describe the situation that caused it.

#2

Using relaxation and breathing techniques

Learn relaxation and breathing techniques that can help manage stress.

- **Deep breathing:** Teach the adolescent how to take deep, slow breaths. Ask them to breathe in deeply through the nose, hold their breath for a few seconds, and exhale slowly through the mouth.
- **Progressive muscle relaxation:** Teach the adolescent how to relax each muscle group of their body in turn, starting with the legs and working up to the head.

#3

Developing coping strategies

Learn to develop coping strategies to manage stress in crowded places.

- **Creating a strategic plan:** Help the adolescent create a plan on how they will deal with their anxiety in crowded places. It may include using relaxation techniques, seeking quiet places, and communicating with trusted people.
- **Coping scenarios:** Create scenarios where the adolescent is in crowded places and has to manage their anxiety. Practice the strategies they have developed.

#4

Strengthening self-confidence

Strengthen self-confidence and learn to manage stress with confidence.

- **Positive self-talk:** Teach the adolescent to use positive affirmations when feeling anxious (e.g., "I can handle it," "I'm safe").
- **Successes and challenges:** Discuss with the adolescent their successes in managing anxiety and the challenges they have faced. Emphasize the importance of recognizing their accomplishments.

#5

Support from family and friends

Learn to ask for and receive support from family and friends when feeling stressed.

- **Discussion on support:** Explain to the adolescent that it is normal to ask for support when feeling anxious. Discuss which people in their lives can offer support (e.g., family, friends).
- **Support seeking exercise:** Create scenarios where the adolescent needs to ask for support from someone. Practice with them the phrases they can use.

23

Situation	Feelings	Automatic thoughts	Evidence supporting these thoughts	Evidence against these thoughts	Alternative thoughts	Behavioral response
Sometimes the noise and the crowd overwhelm me, making it difficult to remain calm.	Anxiety, panic.	I can't stand the noise and the crowds. I can't handle it.	I felt my chest tight and my hands shaking in previous similar situations.	On other occasions when I found myself in a crowd, I managed to calm down with deep breathing and short breaks.	I can handle it. I can find a quiet place and take deep breaths.	Practice breathing techniques before going to events. Seek a quiet place as soon as I feel stressed. Focus on positive thoughts and remind myself that I can get through it.

Identifying the situation:

Identify specific situations where they feel anxious and panicky at social events.

Feelings:

Write down their feelings during these situations.

Automatic thoughts:

Identify their immediate negative thoughts when facing such situations.

Evidence supporting these thoughts:

Identify why they made these thoughts.

Evidence against these thoughts:

Think about why these thoughts may be false.

Alternative thoughts:

Develop positive and constructive thoughts to replace negative ones.

Behavioral response:

Plan specific actions they can take to improve their self-confidence and manage their anxiety at social events.

24

Navigating public transportation

Useful tips

In a similar situation:

Mind the personal space: When choosing a seat, make sure you don't touch those around you. For example, when you sit, make sure your hands and bag don't disturb others.

Observe the reactions of others: If someone seems annoyed or resentful, try to understand the reason. For example, if someone moves away from you, it may be because of their personal space.

Listen carefully to the tone of voice: Try to understand if someone is disturbed by their tone of voice. For example, if someone asks you to move your bag in an intense tone, it means they are probably annoyed.

Apologize if you accidentally touch someone: If you accidentally touch someone, immediately apologize. For example, say, "I'm sorry, I didn't mean it."

Move your bag when the bus is full: If the bus starts to fill up, put your bag on your lap to give others room. That way, you'll avoid conflicts.

Ask if you don't understand: If you don't understand why someone is annoyed, you can politely ask. For example, say, "I'm sorry, what would you like me to do?" It shows that you want to fix the situation.

Story

Peter gets on the bus, not knowing where to sit. He chooses a seat next to a stranger and accidentally touches him, causing discomfort. When the bus is full, someone asks Peter to move his bag, but he doesn't understand the annoyed tone and feels confused.

- Have you ever felt uncomfortable or confused when you didn't know where to sit in a public place? What did you do in that situation?
- How would you feel if someone made a remark in an annoyed tone without understanding why? Have you been in a similar situation?
- How would you react if you accidentally caused discomfort to a stranger on a bus?

#1

Understanding social cues

Learn to recognize and understand social cues and informal rules in public places.

- **Discussion on social cues:** Discuss what social cues are and how to recognize them (e.g., body language, tone of voice, facial expressions).
- **Role-playing:** Role-play situations where you use different social cues and ask the adolescent to identify them. You can practice in situations such as choosing a seat on a bus or reacting to remarks.

#2

Managing social situations

Learn how to manage social situations that cause stress or confusion.

- **Social situations scenarios:** Create scenarios where the adolescent is in public places and has to choose where to sit or react to remarks. Practice appropriate responses.
- **Situation analysis:** Discuss what went well and what could be improved in each scenario. Identify challenges and find solutions.

#3

Strengthening self-confidence and awareness

Strengthen self-confidence and learn to be sensitive to the reactions of others.

- **Positive self-talk:** Teach the adolescent to use positive affirmations in social situations (e.g., "I can handle it," "I am capable of reacting appropriately").
- **Reaction analysis:** Discuss with the adolescent how to recognize and react to the reactions of others. You can use examples and analyze how he or she may react to different situations.

#4

Using relaxation and breathing techniques

Learn relaxation and breathing techniques that can help manage stress in public places.

- **Deep Breathing:** Teach the adolescent how to take deep, slow breaths to calm down when feeling anxious. Ask them to practice this technique in everyday situations.
- **Progressive muscle relaxation:** Teach the adolescent how to relax each muscle group of their body in turn, starting with the legs and working up to the head.

#5

Support from family and friends

Learn to ask for and receive support from family and friends when feeling anxious or confused.

- **Discussion on support:** Explain to the adolescent that it is normal to ask for support when feeling anxious or confused. Discuss which people in their life can offer support (e.g., family, friends).
- **Support seeking exercise:** Create scenarios where the adolescent needs to ask for support from someone. Practice with them on the phrases they can use.

24 Treatment plan

Situation	Feelings	Automatic thoughts	Evidence supporting these thoughts	Evidence against these thoughts	Alternative thoughts	Behavioral response
I got on the bus and I didn't know where to sit, what to do and how to behave.	Anxiety, confusion.	I don't know how to react properly. I don't understand why the other person is upset.	I feel uncomfortable on public transport and I don't always understand other people's reactions.	On other occasions I managed to find a seat without causing discomfort to others.	I can politely ask for instructions or help when I am not sure. I can observe the reactions of others to better understand the situation.	Ask for help or guidance when I am not sure. Try to observe the expressions and tone of voice of others to better understand their needs.

Identifying the situation:

Identify specific situations where they feel anxious and confused.

Feelings:

Write down their feelings during these situations.

Automatic thoughts:

Identify their immediate negative thoughts when facing such situations.

Evidence supporting these thoughts:

Identify why they made these thoughts.

Evidence against these thoughts:

Think about why these thoughts may be false.

Alternative thoughts:

Develop positive and constructive thoughts to replace negative ones.

Behavioral response:

Plan specific actions they can take to improve their self-confidence and manage anxiety and confusion in social situations.

25

Accepting different opinions

Useful tips

In a similar situation:

Listen carefully: When someone disagrees with you, listen carefully to their arguments.

Keep an open mind: Remember that it is normal to have different opinions. Try to see the other person's point of view. For example, think, "I might hear something I hadn't thought of."

Express your point of view calmly: Instead of getting frustrated, talk about your point of view in a calm and polite way. For example, say, "I think that ..."

Ask for an explanation: If you don't understand the other point of view, ask for an explanation. For example, say, "Can you explain how ...?"

See the discussion as an opportunity for learning: See disagreement as an opportunity to learn something new. For example, say, "Can I learn more about ..."

Agree to disagree: It's okay to not always agree. You can say, "Let's agree to disagree, but it's good to have different opinions."

Story

During a class discussion on environmental issues, Anne firmly states that recycling is the best solution. When a classmate argues that reducing waste is more important, Anne feels frustrated and confused. She cannot understand why anyone would disagree with her viewpoint.

- Have you ever felt frustration or confusion when someone disagreed with an opinion of yours? If so, how did you handle it?
- How would you react if someone disagreed with your point of view in a class discussion?

Objectives:	Activities:

#1

Recognizing and understanding disagreements

Learn to recognize and understand the importance of disagreements.

- **Discussion on disagreements:** Discuss what disagreements are and why they are normal in a conversation. Explain that disagreements can help develop and understand different perspectives.
- **Identifying different views:** Give examples from everyday life where people have different views and discuss how these differences can lead to positive changes.

#2

Managing emotions

Learn to manage their emotions when someone disagrees with their point of view.

- **Emotions journal:** Ask the adolescent to keep a journal recording times when they felt frustrated or confused when someone disagreed with their point of view. Discuss with them what they learned from these experiences.
- **Relaxation techniques:** Teach the adolescent relaxation techniques, such as deep breathing or progressive muscle relaxation, to use when they feel anxious or frustrated in a conversation.

#3

Developing conversation skills

Learn to express opinions respectfully and listen to the views of others.

- **Role-playing:** Role-play situations where the adolescent is involved in a conversation and someone disagrees with their point of view. Practice expressing their opinions respectfully and listening to the opinions of others.
- **Situation analysis:** Discuss what went well and what could be improved in each discussion. Identify challenges and find solutions.

#4

Strengthening self-confidence

Strengthen self-confidence and learn to handle disagreements with confidence.

- **Positive self-talk:** Teach the adolescent to use positive affirmations when participating in conversations (e.g., "I can express my opinion respectfully," "Disagreements are normal and helpful").
- **Successes and challenges:** Discuss with the adolescent their successes in discussions and the challenges they have faced. Emphasize the importance of acknowledging their accomplishments.

#5

Support from family and friends

Learn to ask for and receive support from family and friends when feeling frustrated or confused in conversations.

- **Talk about support:** Explain to the adolescent that it is normal to ask for support when they feel frustrated or confused. Discuss which people in their life can offer support (e.g., family, friends).
- **Support seeking exercise:** Create scenarios where the adolescent needs to ask for support from someone. Practice with them the phrases they can use.

25

Treatment plan

Situation	Feelings	Automatic thoughts	Evidence supporting these thoughts	Evidence against these thoughts	Alternative thoughts	Behavioral response
Sometimes I find it hard to understand why someone might have a different opinion. _____ _____ _____ _____ _____ _____ _____	Disappoint-ment, confusion. _____ _____ _____ _____ _____ _____ _____ _____	I don't understand why anyone would disagree with my point of view. My point of view is correct. _____ _____ _____ _____ _____	I have many arguments to convince others that my point of view is correct. _____ _____ _____ _____ _____	But the arguments of others are also important. _____ _____ _____ _____ _____ _____	Different views can coexist. I can listen and learn from other approaches. _____ _____ _____ _____ _____	Show respect for the opinions of others and try to understand their reasoning. Express my own opinion with arguments and be open to discussion. _____

Identifying the situation:

Identify and understand specific situations where they feel frustrated and confused by hearing different opinions.

Feelings:

Write down their feelings during these situations.

Automatic thoughts:

Identify their immediate negative thoughts when facing such situations.

Evidence supporting these thoughts:

Identify why they made these thoughts.

Evidence against these thoughts:

Think about why these thoughts may be false.

Alternative thoughts:

Develop positive and constructive thoughts to replace negative ones.

Behavioral response:

Plan specific actions they can take to improve their understanding and acceptance of different views.

26

Responding to invitations

Useful tips

In a similar situation:

Give a timely response: When you receive an invitation, try to respond as soon as possible. You can say, "Thanks for the invitation! I will come to the party."

Explain your feelings: If you feel nervous about the social event, explain it to your friend. You can say, "I'm feeling a little nervous about the party, but I really want to come and try."

Ask for help if you need it: If you don't know how to respond, ask a parent or friend for help. You can say, "I received an invitation to a party, and I don't know how to respond. What would you suggest?"

Suggest an alternative: If you can't go, suggest an alternative. You can say, "I can't come to the party, but I'd like to celebrate with you at another time."

Express yourself politely: Even if you decide not to go, respond politely. Say, "Thank you so much for the invitation, but I won't be able to come."

Learn from experience: Recognize what went wrong and try to fix it in the future. You can tell yourself, "Next time I will respond immediately to the invitation and explain how I feel."

Story

Sarah receives an invitation to a birthday party, but she isn't sure how to respond. She feels nervous about the social event, but she doesn't want to disappoint her friend. Not knowing what to do, Sarah ignores the invitation. On the day of the party, her friend asks Sarah why she hasn't responded. Sarah realizes she didn't handle the situation well.

- How do you think Sarah felt? Have you ever felt anxious about a social event and had difficulty deciding what to do?
- What do you think Sarah thought when her friend asked her why she hadn't responded to the invitation? Have you ever been in a situation where you felt uncomfortable because you didn't respond to someone?
- How could Sarah better handle the situation the next time she receives an invitation? What would you do if you didn't know how to respond to an invitation?

26

Objectives:	Activities:

#1

Recognizing and understanding anxiety about social events

Learn to recognize and understand the anxiety caused by social events.

- **Discussion on anxiety:** Discuss what anxiety is and how it can occur in social situations. Use examples from everyday life.
- **Journal:** Ask the adolescent to record the times they feel anxious about social events and describe the situation that caused it.

#2

Developing skills for responding to social invitations

Learn to respond to social invitations with confidence.

- **Role-playing:** Create scenarios where the adolescent receives a social invitation and has to decide how to respond. Practice appropriate responses.
- **A response plan:** Help the adolescent create a plan for responding to invitations. It may include assessing the situation and using polite phrases such as "Thanks for the invitation. I would love to come, but I have another commitment."

#3

Managing stress for social situations

Learn techniques to manage stress caused by social situations.

- **Relaxation techniques:** Teach the adolescent relaxation techniques, such as deep breathing or progressive muscle relaxation, to use before social events.
- **Preparing for the event:** Help the adolescent prepare for the social event. It may include choosing clothes, preparing for conversations, and practicing relaxation techniques.

#4

Strengthening self-confidence and social skills

Boost self-confidence and improve social skills.

- **Positive self-talk:** Teach the adolescent to use positive affirmations when preparing for social events (e.g., "I can handle it," "I'm capable of enjoying the party").
- **Participate in social activities:** Encourage the adolescent to participate in small social activities to practice their skills and feel more comfortable at bigger events.

#5

Support from family and friends

Learn to ask for and receive support from family and friends when they feel anxious about social events.

- **Talk about support:** Explain to the adolescent that it's normal to ask for support when feeling anxious about social events. Discuss which people in their life can offer support (e.g., family, friends).
- **Support-seeking exercise:** Create scenarios where the adolescent needs to ask for support from someone. Practice the phrases they can use.

26

Treatment plan

Situation	Feelings	Automatic thoughts	Evidence supporting these thoughts	Evidence against these thoughts	Alternative thoughts	Behavioral response
I don't want to disappoint my friends, but sometimes I don't know how to behave and it looks like I'm ignoring them.	Anxiety, embarrassment, guilt.	I don't know what to say. If I go, I'll feel uncomfortable. If I don't go, I'll disappoint my friend.	I didn't respond to the invitation because I felt nervous.	My friend would like to know if I'm going to the party. My response can be simple and honest.	I can respond to the invitation honestly. I can explain to my friend how I feel and ask for understanding.	Explain how I feel to my friends and ask for understanding. I can try to go to social events, even if I feel a little anxious.

Identifying the situation:

Identify and understand specific situations where they feel anxious and embarrassed when receiving social invitations.

Feelings:

Write down their feelings during these situations.

Automatic thoughts:

Identify their immediate negative thoughts when facing such situations.

Evidence supporting these thoughts:

Identify why they made these thoughts.

Evidence against these thoughts:

Think about why these thoughts may be false.

Alternative thoughts:

Develop positive and constructive thoughts to replace negative ones.

Behavioral response:

Plan specific actions to improve their self-confidence and manage their anxiety.

27

Recognizing different social roles

In a similar situation:

Use professional language: Instead of saying "Hey, man!", say "Good morning, Mr/Mrs [Surname]. Nice to meet you".

Observe your colleagues: See how other employees address the boss and follow their example. This will help you understand the appropriate language and behavior.

Ask for guidance: If you're not sure how to speak, ask a more experienced colleague: "What is the best way to address our boss?"

Learn from your mistakes: Acknowledge your mistake and try to correct it. Say "Sorry about before. I will try to use more polite speech in the future."

Show respect to everyone: Be polite and show respect to all your colleagues, not just the boss. Say "Good morning, how are you today?"

Be prepared: Think about how you will speak before you address someone, especially superiors. Think "What is the appropriate way to greet my boss?" and prepare a formal greeting.

Story

Alex is excited to meet all the staff members in his new part-time job. On his first day, he greets his boss with a simple "Hey, man!" as he would with his friends. His boss is annoyed and reminds him to be more polite. Alex feels confused and embarrassed.

- What do you think of Alex greeting his boss in such a casual way? Have you ever used inappropriate language in a formal situation?
- What do you think Alex thought when his boss reminded him to use more polite language? Have you ever been in a situation where someone pointed out that you should be more polite?
- How do you think Alex could have handled the situation better? What would you do if you were in his position?

Objectives:	Activities:

#1

Understanding professional expectations

Learn to recognize and understand professional expectations and behavioral patterns.

- **Discussion on professional expectations:** Discuss appropriate standards of behavior and language in professional settings. Use examples to explain the differences between friendly and professional communication.
- **Situation analysis:** Give examples from everyday life where professional behavior is required and ask the adolescent to analyze how they should behave in each situation.

#2

Practicing appropriate language

Learn to use appropriate language and behavior in professional environments.

- **Role-playing:** Create scenarios where the adolescent has to interact with colleagues and supervisors in a professional environment. Practice using polite phrases and adhering to professional standards.
- **Workplace relationships analysis:** Discuss the differences between relationships with friends and relationships with co-workers and supervisors. Identify challenges and find solutions.

#3

Managing emotions

Learn to manage emotions when faced with comments or corrections from superiors.

- **Emotions journal:** Ask the adolescent to record times when they feel confused or embarrassed by comments from superiors. Discuss what they learned from these experiences.
- **Relaxation techniques:** Teach the adolescent relaxation techniques, such as deep breathing or progressive muscle relaxation, to use when feeling anxious or uncomfortable in professional situations.

#4

Developing confidence and professional skills

Enhance self-confidence and develop professional skills.

- **Positive self-talk:** Teach the adolescent to use positive affirmations when facing professional challenges (e.g., "I can learn and improve," "I am capable of adapting to professional environments").
- **Participate in professional activities:** Encourage the adolescent to participate in professional activities, such as seminars or workshops, to improve their professional skills and become more comfortable in professional environments.

#5

Support from family and friends

Learn to ask for and receive support from family and friends when facing challenges in their professional life.

- **Talk about support:** Explain to the adolescent that it's normal to ask for support when facing challenges in their professional life. Discuss which people in their life can offer support (e.g., family, friends, mentors).
- **Support-seeking exercise:** Create scenarios where the adolescent must seek support or advice from someone. Practice the phrases they can use.

27

Situation	Feelings	Automatic thoughts	Evidence supporting these thoughts	Evidence against these thoughts	Alternative thoughts	Behavioral response
I sometimes find it difficult to use appropriate language in different situations.	Confusion, embarrassment.	I didn't realize it was a mistake. I don't know how to talk properly.	My boss got annoyed and told me to use more polite language.	Professional circumstances require a different language than friendly situations. Most people learn to adapt their language to the situation.	I can learn to use more professional language. It's normal to make mistakes at first and learn from them.	Observe how my colleagues speak and adapt. Ask for guidance and clarification if I am not sure of the correct way of speaking.

Identifying the situation:

Identify and understand specific situations where they feel confused and embarrassed when dealing with professional circumstances.

Feelings:

Write down their feelings during these situations.

Automatic thoughts:

Identify their immediate negative thoughts when facing such situations.

Evidence supporting these thoughts:

Identify why they made these thoughts.

Evidence against these thoughts:

Think about why these thoughts may be false.

Alternative thoughts:

Develop positive and constructive thoughts to replace negative ones.

Behavioral response:

Plan specific actions they can take to improve their self-confidence and manage their anxiety and embarrassment in professional circumstances.

28

Volunteering and social engagement

Useful tips

In a similar situation:

Ask for clear instructions: If you feel confused about tasks, approach the person in charge and say, "Can you explain again what I need to do?"

Break tasks into small steps: If the task seems too big, break it into smaller pieces. Tell yourself, "First, I will..."

Engage in small conversations: If you feel uncomfortable in conversations, start with small talk. You can say, "This is the first time I've ever participated in something like this. How about you?"

Find a volunteer partner: Find another volunteer who works alone and say, "Do you want to work together? We can be more effective that way."

Develop a plan of action: Plan how you will spend your day. Tell yourself, "I'm going to start with... and then I'm going to take a little break."

Don't hesitate to ask for help: If you're feeling lost, approach a volunteer and say, "I need some help figuring out what I need to do. Can you help me?"

Story

During a beach clean-up event, Daniel feels overwhelmed by the many participants and all the different tasks he is assigned to do. When he ends up in a group of chatty volunteers, he finds engaging in their conversations and following instructions challenging. Feeling out of place, Daniel begins picking up trash on his own, avoiding interaction.

- How do you think Daniel felt? Have you ever been in a similar situation?
- What do you think about Daniel's decision to avoid interaction with the group? Have you ever felt out of place in a group? If yes, what did you do?

Objectives:	Activities:

#1

Understanding and managing stress in group activities

Learn to recognize and manage stress caused by group activities.

- **Journal:** Ask the adolescent to record the times they feel anxious in group activities and describe the situation that caused it. Discuss with them what they learned from these experiences.
- **Relaxation techniques:** Teach the adolescent relaxation techniques, such as deep breathing or progressive muscle relaxation, to use before and during group activities.

#2

Practicing social skills

Improve social interaction skills and feel more comfortable in group activities.

- **Role-playing:** Create scenarios where the adolescent participates in group activities and has to interact with others. Practice appropriate responses and participation in discussions.
- **Group activities:** Encourage the adolescent to participate in smaller group activities to practice skills and become more comfortable in larger events.

#3

Strengthening self-confidence

Boost self-confidence and learn to manage embarrassment in social situations.

- **Positive self-talk:** Teach the adolescent to use positive affirmations when participating in group activities (e.g., "I can handle it," "I am capable of participating in the group").
- **Acknowledging successes:** Discuss the adolescent's successes in group activities and the challenges they have faced. Emphasize the importance of recognizing their achievements.

#4

Developing coping strategies

Learn to develop strategies for coping with stress and embarrassment in group activities.

- **Strategic Plan:** Help the adolescent create a plan about how they will deal with their anxiety in group activities. It may include using relaxation techniques, seeking quiet places, and communicating with trusted people.
- **Coping scenarios:** Create scenarios where the adolescent is in group activities and needs to manage their anxiety. Practice the strategies they have developed.

#5

Support from family and friends

Learn to ask for and receive support from family and friends when they feel anxious or embarrassed in group activities.

- **Talk about support:** Explain to the adolescent that it's normal to ask for support when feeling anxious or uncomfortable in group activities. Discuss which people in their life can offer support (e.g., family, friends).
- **Support-seeking exercise:** Create scenarios where the adolescent needs to ask for support from someone. Practice the phrases they can use.

28

Treatment plan

Situation	Feelings	Automatic thoughts	Evidence supporting these thoughts	Evidence against these thoughts	Alternative thoughts	Behavioral response
Sometimes I find it difficult to participate in discussions and follow multiple instructions. ___ ___ ___ ___ ___ ___ ___	Anxiety, embarrassment, overwhelmed. ___ ___ ___ ___ ___ ___ ___ ___	I can't follow the conversations. I don't know what to do. I don't belong here. ___ ___ ___ ___ ___ ___	I found it difficult to participate in the conversations and follow the instructions. ___ ___ ___	In other situations I was able to find my role and participate successfully. I can ask for help and guidance when I feel lost. ___ ___	I can ask for help when I feel lost. I don't have to be in all the conversations to belong. I can find a way to contribute that works for me. ___ ___	Ask for help and guidance when I feel lost. Try to participate in small groups and seek opportunities to contribute in a way that I feel comfortable with.

Identifying the situation:

Identify and understand specific situations where they feel anxious and uncomfortable when at social events with many people and many tasks.

Feelings:

Write down their feelings during these situations.

Automatic thoughts:

Identify their immediate negative thoughts when facing such situations.

Evidence supporting these thoughts:

Identify why they made these thoughts.

Evidence against these thoughts:

Think about why these thoughts may be false.

Alternative thoughts:

Develop positive and constructive thoughts to replace negative ones.

Behavioral response:

Plan specific actions they can take to improve their self-confidence and manage their anxiety in social situations.

29

Authority figures

Useful tips

In a similar situation:

Use polite language: Instead of saying, "Watch where you're going," say, "Sorry, I didn't see you." It shows respect and politeness.

Apologize immediately: If you realize you have made a mistake, apologize immediately. You can say, "I am sorry for my carelessness."

Show respect for the authorities: Remember that police officers and other authorities deserve respect. Say, "Good morning, officer," or "Good morning to you."

Think before you speak: Before you say something, think about how the other person might take it. Ask yourself, "Is what I'm saying polite?"

Learn from your experiences: Use this experience to learn and improve your behavior in the future. Tell yourself, "I will pay more attention to how I talk to others."

Ask for guidance if needed: If you are not sure how to talk to someone, ask a parent or teacher. You can say, "What is the best way to talk to a police officer?"

Story

During a school field trip, Marc accidentally bumps into a policeman and casually says, "Watch where you're going." The policeman, with a surprised look on his face, explains that Marc should show more respect. Marc feels embarrassed and confused about what he did wrong.

- Have you ever been in a similar situation where someone implied you were disrespectful?
- How do you think Marc felt when the police officer told him to show more respect? Have you ever felt embarrassed or confused about something you said or did by mistake?
- Do you think Marc understood what he did wrong? How would you react if someone told you that you should show more respect?

29

#1

Understanding the importance of respect and politeness

Learn to recognize and understand the importance of respect in all interactions.

- **Discussion on respect:** Discuss what respect means and why it's important. Use examples from everyday life to explain how respect affects relationships and interactions.
- **Recognize respect:** Ask the adolescent to identify situations where they or someone else showed respect. Discuss how these situations have had a positive impact.

#2

Strengthening empathy

Understand the concept of empathy and how to apply it in everyday interactions.

- **Discussion on empathy:** Discuss what empathy means and why it's important. Use examples where empathy helped someone feel better or resolve a disagreement.
- **Role-playing:** Role-play different situations where empathy is needed. Ask the adolescent to put themselves in the other person's shoes and express how they would feel or react.

#3

Developing social skills

Develop social skills and learn how to interact with respect and courtesy.

- **Discussion on social skills:** Discuss basic social skills (such as saying "please" and "thank you") and why they are important.
- **Watching and analyzing:** Watch videos or movie scenes together and discuss the social interactions you observed. Analyze how they could be more polite and respectful.

#4

Recognizing and expressing emotions

Learn to recognize and express emotions in an appropriate way.

- **Discussion on feelings:** Discuss the different emotions (joy, sadness, anger) and how we express them respectfully to others.
- **Feelings journal:** Ask the adolescent to keep a journal where they write daily about how they felt and why. Discuss how they express these feelings in their interactions.

#5

Strengthening self-esteem

Build self-esteem and learn to respect themselves and others.

- **Discussion on self-esteem:** Discuss what self-esteem is and why it's important. Explain how respect for oneself is connected to respect for others.
- **Strengths recognition exercise:** Ask the adolescent to list their strengths and talents. Discuss how they can use these strengths to help others and show respect.

29

Treatment plan

Situation	Feelings	Automatic thoughts	Evidence supporting these thoughts	Evidence against these thoughts	Alternative thoughts	Behavioral response
Sometimes it seems that I don't show respect to others, but the truth is that I don't realize it at the time. ___ ___ ___ ___ ___	Embarrass-ment, confusion. ___ ___ ___ ___ ___ ___ ___ ___ ___	I didn't do anything wrong. The officer shouldn't have taken it the wrong way. ___ ___ ___ ___ ___	I had no intention of showing disrespect. I just spoke carelessly. ___ ___ ___ ___ ___ ___ ___	In many social situations it's important to show respect, especially to people of authority such as police officers. ___ ___ ___	It's important to use a polite tone and language, especially with strangers and people of authority. I can learn to communicate better with respect. ___ ___	Practice polite and respectful communication, recognize social expectations and strive to show respect to all, regardless of position. ___

Identifying the situation:

Identify and understand specific situations where they feel embarrassed and confused by social interactions.

Feelings:

Write down their feelings during these situations.

Automatic thoughts:

Identify their immediate thoughts when facing such situations.

Evidence supporting these thoughts:

Identify why they made these thoughts.

Evidence against these thoughts:

Think about why these thoughts may be false.

Alternative thoughts:

Develop positive and constructive thoughts to replace negative ones.

Behavioral response:

Plan specific actions they can take to improve their communication in social situations.

30

Interpretation of social rules and conventions

Useful tips

In a similar situation:

Wait your turn to speak: When someone else is speaking, wait until they are finished before you say anything. Think "I'll wait until my cousin finishes his ideas before I say anything."

Be respectful of other people's conversations: If the conversation is not about your favorite game, try to join the conversation or listen. Say: "Let's talk about my game later. Now I'll listen to the conversation."

Take notes if you have something important to say: If you think of something you want to share, keep it in mind or write it down for later. Say: "I'll keep this thought and share it when it's my turn."

Observe others' reactions: If others seem annoyed or frustrated, adjust your behavior. Think "Others seem annoyed. I will wait before speaking again."

Apologize if necessary: If you realize you interrupted, apologize. Say: "I'm sorry for interrupting you. I'll wait my turn."

Show interest in others: Instead of just talking about your favorite game, ask others about their interests. Say: "What did you do today? Tell me more about it."

Story

At a family dinner, Ryan keeps interrupting conversations to randomly say things about his favorite video game. His cousins seem annoyed, and his aunt politely reminds him to wait his turn to speak. Ryan feels embarrassed by their reactions.

- How do you think Ryan felt? Have you ever been in a similar situation where you felt embarrassed?
- What do you think Ryan could have done to participate in the conversation without interrupting the others? How would you react if you wanted to say something but the others were talking?
- How do you think Ryan's relatives could react to help him feel more comfortable and participate in the conversation? What would you want them to say in a similar situation to make you feel better?

Objectives:	Activities:

#1

Understanding the importance of communication

Understand the importance of a smooth communication flow and how to contribute to it.

- **Talk about communication:** Discuss what good communication means and why it's important in social interactions. Use examples from everyday life.
- **Role-playing:** Role-play different communication situations where the adolescent has to wait their turn to speak.

#2

Developing listening skills

Learn to listen actively and show interest in what others are saying.

- **Talk about listening:** Discuss what active listening means and how the adolescent can show that they are really listening to someone.
- **Listening exercises:** Do exercises where the adolescent has to listen to a story or conversation and repeat what they heard, showing that they were listening.

#3

Enhancing empathy and understanding of others' feelings

Develop the ability to understand and respect the feelings of others.

- **Talk about empathy:** Discuss what empathy is and how the adolescent can show it in their everyday interactions.
- **Situation analysis:** Analyze situations where others felt annoyed and discuss how the adolescent could show more understanding and respect.

#4

Understanding the importance of turn-taking in conversations

Learn to recognize the importance of waiting for their turn to speak in discussions.

- **Talk about taking turns when speaking:** Talk about how conversations work and why it's important not to interrupt others.
- **Conversation exercises:** Role-play conversations where the adolescent has to wait their turn to speak. Reward them when they get it right.

#5

Strengthening self-esteem and self-confidence

Boost self-esteem and confidence to feel comfortable and secure in conversations.

- **Discuss self-esteem:** Discuss the importance of self-esteem and how it relates to how the adolescent communicates with others.
- **Strengths recognition exercises:** Ask them to identify their strengths and positive attributes and discuss how these can help them feel more comfortable and communicate better.

30 Treatment plan

Situation	Feelings	Automatic thoughts	Evidence supporting these thoughts	Evidence against these thoughts	Alternative thoughts	Behavioral response
Sometimes I interrupt people when they are talking and I am not a good listener.	Embarrass-ment.	I want to talk about something I like. I don't understand why it's wrong to interrupt.	I talked about something I like.	My cousins looked annoyed. My aunt told me to wait my turn.	I can wait until the conversation is over before I speak. It's important to listen to others before speaking.	Wait for my turn to speak and try to participate in other people's conversations without interrupting.

Identifying the situation:

Identify specific situations where they feel embarrassed after interrupting conversations.

Feelings:

Write down their feelings during these situations.

Automatic thoughts:

Identify their immediate thoughts when facing such situations.

Evidence supporting these thoughts:

Identify why they made these thoughts.

Evidence against these thoughts:

Think about why these thoughts may be false.

Alternative thoughts:

Develop positive and constructive thoughts to replace negative ones.

Behavioral response:

Plan specific actions they can take to improve their understanding and response to such situations.

31

Conversation in different contexts

© Upbility Publications

In a similar situation:

Observe the flow of the conversation: Before you speak, take a moment to observe what others are saying. If they are talking about weekend plans, you might say, "What are you planning to do this weekend?"

Connect with their subject: Try to link your comment to the subject of the conversation. Say, "This weekend I'm thinking of watching a documentary about space. Do you guys have anything interesting planned?"

Use questions to engage: If you're not sure what to say, ask questions. Say: "What are your plans for the weekend? Do you have anything fun planned?"

Keep your comment short and relevant: Try to say something short and relevant to the topic. Say, "This weekend I'm going to the movies. What are you guys doing?"

Show interest in other people's plans: Show interest in your classmates' plans. Say, "Your plan for the weekend sounds great. Tell me more about it."

Learn from experience: Use this experience to improve your social skills. Think: "Next time, I'll try to link my comment to the conversation better."

Story

During a school recess, Mary sees her classmates discussing about their weekend plans. She wants to participate but isn't sure how to do that. When she finally says, "I saw a documentary about space," the group falls silent, not knowing how to respond. Mary feels embarrassed and leaves the conversation.

- How do you think Mary felt when her classmates fell silent after she told them about the documentary? Have you ever felt anything similar?
- What do you think Mary could do to feel more comfortable when she wants to participate in a conversation? What would you do if you were in her shoes?
- How do you think Mary's classmates could react to make her feel more welcome in the conversation?

Objectives:

Activities:

#1

Understanding the importance of relevance

Learn to make comments that are relevant to the current topic of discussion.

- **Conversation about relevance:** Discuss why it's important to stay on topic and how to do this.
- **Relevance exercises:** Provide examples of conversations and ask the adolescent to add comments that are relevant to the topic being discussed.

#2

Strengthening confidence in social interactions

Enhance their confidence in social interactions to feel comfortable participating in conversations.

- **Discussion on self-confidence:** Discuss the importance of self-confidence in social interactions and how it affects participation in conversations.
- **Confidence exercise:** Ask the adolescent to list their strengths and positive attributes and discuss how these can help them feel more comfortable in conversations.

#3

Developing active listening skills

Learn to listen actively and understand the topic of the discussion before participating.

- **Talk about active listening:** Discuss what active listening means and how to show that you are really listening to someone.
- **Active listening exercises:** Do exercises where the adolescent has to listen to a story or conversation and repeat what they heard, showing that they understand the topic before adding their comment.

#4

Developing group integration skills

Learn how to integrate smoothly into a discussion or group and make comments confidently.

- **Discuss group integration:** Discuss how the adolescent can smoothly join a discussion and when it's appropriate to speak.
- **Role-playing:** Role-play various situations where the adolescent must join a conversation and add comments confidently.

#5

Understanding and expressing interests

Learn to express their interests in a way that is relevant to the current conversation.

- **Discussion of interests:** Discuss ways in which the adolescent can link their interests to the current conversation (e.g., ask others if they have seen something similar or if they are interested in the topic).
- **Discussion exercises:** Plan discussions where the adolescent should integrate their interests in a relevant way.

31

Treatment plan

Situation	Feelings	Automatic thoughts	Evidence supporting these thoughts	Evidence against these thoughts	Alternative thoughts	Behavioral response
I want to participate in discussions with my classmates, but I'm not sure how to do that. _____ _____ _____ _____ _____ _____	Embarrass-ment, rejection. _____ _____ _____ _____ _____ _____	I don't know how to participate in the conversa-tions. The others don't want me to join in. _____ _____ _____ _____ _____	When I spoke, the group fell silent and I felt embarrassed. _____ _____ _____ _____ _____	Sometimes I have managed to participate in discussions successfully. My classmates may not have known what to say about space. _____	I can try to find common topics of discussion. The group may not have known how to continue the discussion about space. _____ _____ _____ _____	Try to rejoin the conversation by asking about the weekend plans or mentioning something relevant to the topic they are discussing. Observe the reactions and adjust my comments accordingly.

Identifying the situation:

Identify specific situations where they feel uncomfortable and find it difficult to participate in discussions.

Feelings:

Write down their feelings during these situations.

Automatic thoughts:

Identify their immediate thoughts that may prevent them from participating effectively in discussions.

Evidence supporting these thoughts:

Identify why they made these thoughts.

Evidence against these thoughts:

Think about why these thoughts may be false.

Alternative thoughts:

Develop positive and constructive thoughts to replace negative ones.

Behavioral response:

Plan specific actions they can take to improve their ability to participate in conversations and feel more comfortable in social interactions.

32

Navigating transactions

Useful tips

In a similar situation:

Make eye contact: When you approach the cashier, try to make eye contact. This shows respect and attention. Say "Good morning" while looking the cashier in the eyes.

Greet politely: When you approach the cashier, say "Good morning" or "Good evening". This shows politeness and makes the interaction more pleasant.

Answer questions: If the cashier asks you a question, try to answer it. Say "Yes, I found everything okay, thank you".

Thank the salesperson: When the transaction is complete, say "Thank you very much" or "Have a nice day". This shows appreciation for the service.

Use a polite tone: Speak in a polite and calm tone. Say "I'd like this book, please" when handing the book to the cashier.

Practice: Try to practice polite interaction with salespeople. Think "Today I will try to be polite to the cashier at the bookstore."

Story

In the bookstore, Tyler approaches the cashier with a book but does not make eye contact. When the cashier asks him if everything is okay, Tyler does not answer and instead places the money on the counter without saying a word. Confused, the cashier completes the transaction. Later, Tyler's mom explains to him how greeting and thanking a store clerk is the polite thing to do.

- How do you feel when you have to talk to a clerk or cashier at the store? What can you do to feel more comfortable?
- Why is it important to greet and thank store clerks when they assist us?
- What small phrases or words can you use to be kind to someone assisting you with a purchase?

32

#1

Understanding the importance of politeness during transactions

Understand the importance of politeness during transactions and learn how to greet and thank store clerks.

- **Talk about politeness:** Discuss why it's important to greet and thank store employees. Give examples from everyday life.
- **Role-playing:** Role-play with the adolescent situations where they play the role of the customer and you play the role of the clerk. Practice greeting and saying "thank you" during the transaction.

#2

Developing eye contact

Learn the importance of eye contact and practice it during transactions.

- **Talk about eye contact:** Explain why eye contact is important in interactions with others. Discuss how it can make others feel more comfortable and show respect.
- **Eye contact exercises:** Practice exercises where the adolescent must maintain eye contact for a few seconds while talking to you or someone else.

#3

Developing verbal communication skills

Learn to answer a clerk's questions and use basic polite language.

- **Talk about verbal communication:** Discuss the basic phrases we use in interactions, such as "hello," "thank you," and "please."
- **Communication exercises:** Create scenarios where the adolescent will have to answer questions and use polite language. Practice until they feel comfortable.

#4

Developing active listening skills

Learn to listen actively and respond appropriately to a clerk's questions.

- **Talk about active listening:** Discuss the importance of active listening and how the adolescent can show that they are really listening to someone.
- **Listening exercises:** Role-play situations where you are the store clerk and the adolescent is the customer. Practice listening to questions and answering appropriately.

#5

Strengthening confidence in social interactions

Build confidence in social interactions and feel comfortable communicating with store employees.

- **Talk about self-confidence:** Discuss how confidence can help in social interactions and transactions.
- **Confidence exercise:** Ask the adolescent to list their strengths and positive aspects and discuss how these can help them feel more comfortable in transactions. Practice in real-life situations.

32

Treatment plan

Situation	Feelings	Automatic thoughts	Evidence supporting these thoughts	Evidence against these thoughts	Alternative thoughts	Behavioral response
I have a hard time keeping eye contact with the employee when I'm shopping. _____ _____ _____ _____ _____ _____ _____ _____	Anxiety, embarrass-ment. _____ _____ _____ _____ _____ _____ _____ _____	I don't know what to say. It's uncomforta-ble to talk. _____ _____ _____ _____ _____ _____	I did not make eye contact and did not respond to the cashier. _____ _____ _____ _____ _____ _____	The cashier completed the transaction nonetheless. My mom said it's important to say hello and thank you. _____ _____	It 's polite and normal to greet and thank the clerk. I can practice saying thank you and making eye contact. _____ _____	Practice making eye contact and saying thank you to store clerks during transactions. _____ _____ _____

Identifying the situation:

Identify specific situations where they feel anxiety and embarrassment in their social interactions.

Feelings:

Write down their feelings during these situations.

Automatic thoughts:

Identify their immediate thoughts that may prevent polite interaction with others.

Evidence supporting these thoughts:

Identify why they made these thoughts.

Evidence against these thoughts:

Think about why these thoughts may be false.

Alternative thoughts:

Develop positive and constructive thoughts to replace negative ones.

Behavioral response:

Plan specific actions they can take to improve their social skills when shopping.

33

Dealing with emergencies

Useful tips

In a similar situation:

Learn the emergency plan: Ask your teacher about the evacuation plan and find out what the procedure is. Tell yourself, "If the alarm goes off again, I'll know what to do."

Practice evacuation drills: Actively participate in fire drills to familiarize yourself with the process. Tell yourself, "These drills are important so I know how to react in an emergency."

Follow your classmates: If you are not sure what to do, observe your classmates and follow their movements. Tell yourself, "If I see others get in line, I will do the same."

Ask teachers for help: If you feel panicky or don't know what to do, ask a teacher for help. Say, "Can you help me? I'm not sure what to do."

Stay calm: Try to stay calm and take deep breaths if you feel panic. Tell yourself, "If I stay calm, I will be able to react better."

Learn from experience: Use this experience to improve your reaction in the future. Tell yourself, "Next time I will remember to follow the teacher's instructions and get out quickly."

Story

When the fire alarm goes off at school, John freezes in panic, not knowing what to do. His classmates quickly line up to get out, but John stays at his desk in shock. A teacher notices him and gently guides him towards the door, reminding him that it's important to follow the others. When outside, John feels embarrassed that he didn't know how to react.

- What can you do to stay calm when you hear the fire alarm?
- What do you think is important to remember when an emergency occurs at school?
- Have you been in a similar situation?

33

Objectives:	Activities:

#1

Understanding the evacuation process

Understand the steps of the evacuation process to feel prepared in case of an emergency.

- **Educational discussion:** Discuss the evacuation process, explaining the steps to follow during a fire (e.g., stand up, get in line, follow instructions).
- **Visual material:** Use visual supports, such as evacuation maps, to show routes and fire exits.

#2

Developing panic coping skills

Learn techniques to stay calm and react appropriately in emergencies.

- **Discussion on panic:** Discuss what panic is and how it can affect thinking and reaction. Talk about ways to stay calm in stressful situations.
- **Breathing exercises:** Teach the adolescent deep breathing exercises that can help them calm down when they feel panicky.

#3

Taking part in evacuation drills

Actively participate in school evacuation drills to become familiar with the process and feel more prepared.

- **Participate in planned exercises:** Encourage the adolescent to participate in planned school evacuation drills by providing guidance and support.
- **Simulate drills:** Organize simulated evacuation drills at home where the adolescent must follow the evacuation procedure.

#4

Developing confidence in emergencies

Build confidence and belief in their abilities to react appropriately in an emergency.

- **Discussion on confidence:** Discuss how confidence can help in difficult situations and how practicing can make the adolescent feel more confident.
- **Reward effort:** Reward the adolescent each time they successfully participate in an exercise or show signs of improvement in dealing with panic.

#5

Familiarizing with the safety measures and signs

Learn to recognize the signs and safety measures their school has in place.

- **Tour the evacuation routes:** Walk the evacuation routes at school with the adolescent and explain the signs to follow.
- **Signs recognition game:** Create a game where the adolescent has to identify evacuation signs in different parts of the school.

#6

Developing collaboration skills with classmates and teachers

Learn to cooperate with classmates and teachers during evacuation drills.

- **Talk about cooperation:** Discuss the importance of working with others during evacuation drills.
- **Collaboration games:** Play games that reinforce cooperation and teamwork, helping the adolescent feel more comfortable working with others.

33

Treatment plan

Situation	Feelings	Automatic thoughts	Evidence supporting these thoughts	Evidence against these thoughts	Alternative thoughts	Behavioral response
I panic when something unexpected happens and I don't know what to do.	Panic, confusion, embarrass-ment.	I don't know what to do. I can't handle emergencies.	I froze and did not react like my classmates.	The teacher helped me get out safely and figure out what to do.	It's normal to feel panic in emergencies. I can learn and practice to be more prepared next time.	Take part in fire drills and practice the steps of evacuation. Ask teachers or classmates for help if I am unsure.

Identifying the situation:

Identify specific situations where they feel panic and embarrassment in emergencies.

Feelings:

Write down their feelings during these situations.

Automatic thoughts:

Identify their immediate thoughts that may prevent them from reacting effectively in emergencies.

Evidence supporting these thoughts:

Identify why they made these thoughts.

Evidence against these thoughts:

Think about why these thoughts may be false.

Alternative thoughts:

Develop positive and constructive thoughts to replace negative ones.

Behavioral response:

Plan specific actions they can do to improve their alertness and react more effectively in emergencies.

34

Sports spirit

Useful tips

In a similar situation:

Understand the role of the team: Think of the team as a puzzle. Each piece is important to build the complete picture. If everyone works together, the team will function better.

Listen and observe your teammates: When your teammates ask for a pass, it means they are in a good position to help the team. You can say to yourself, "When I hear someone yelling, I need to look around and see if they are in a better position than me."

Share the ball to improve the team: When you share the ball, you give your team more opportunities to score goals. Say to yourself, "If I pass the ball, we might have a better chance to score."

Take the feedback positively: When your coach gives you advice, it means he wants to help you improve. Think "My coach wants the best for me and the team. I will try to follow his advice."

Use visual aids: Ask your coach to show you videos or game plans to help you better understand the importance of passing and teamwork. This can help you see how passing can lead to more goals.

Practice teamwork: During training, ask to do exercises that reinforce teamwork, such as small group games where passing is essential for success. Think "I will practice passing and cooperation to become a better teammate."

Story

During a soccer match, Chris focuses on scoring a goal and ignores his teammates asking for a pass. When he misses a crucial shot, his teammates feel frustrated, but Chris doesn't understand why. After the game, the coach explains to him the importance of teamwork and passing the ball.

- Have you ever ignored your teammates in a match? How did you feel afterward?

- How would you react if you were in Chris' position and your teammates were frustrated with you?

- What do you think about the importance of teamwork on a sports team?

34

Objectives:	Activities:

#1

Understanding the importance of teamwork

Understand the importance of teamwork and how working together can lead to better results.

- **Discuss teamwork:** Discuss what teamwork means and why it's important in sports and other activities. Use examples of successful teams.
- **Role-playing:** Role-play situations where the adolescent has to work with others to achieve a common goal.

#2

Developing communication skills

Learn to communicate effectively with teammates during the game.

- **Discuss communication:** Discuss the importance of communication in sports and how it can improve team performance.
- **Communication exercises:** Do exercises where the adolescent must communicate with teammates to complete an activity.

#3

Practicing joint decision-making

Learn to make decisions together with teammates and take their opinions into account.

- **Discussion on decision-making:** Discuss how shared decision-making can improve team performance and enhance cooperation.
- **Group activities:** Practice group activities where the adolescent has to make decisions with his or her teammates.

#4

Developing sharing skills

Learn to share when necessary.

- **Sharing discussion:** Discuss why it is important to share and how it benefits the team.
- **Sharing exercises:** Do exercises where the adolescent has to share something in different play situations.

#5

Developing empathy and understanding of the reactions of the teammates

Develop the ability to understand the emotions and reactions of teammates.

- **Discussion on empathy:** Discuss what empathy means and how it can help in understanding the feelings of others.
- **Comprehension exercises:** Role-play situations where the adolescent must recognize and respond to the emotions of their teammates during play.

#6

Strengthening self-esteem through cooperation

Boost self-esteem by seeing the positive results of working together with teammates.

- **Discuss self-esteem:** Discuss how working with others can boost self-esteem and a sense of accomplishment.
- **Feedback and reward:** Provide positive feedback and reward whenever the adolescent works effectively with teammates.

34 Treatment plan

Situation	Feelings	Automatic thoughts	Evidence supporting these thoughts	Evidence against these thoughts	Alternative thoughts	Behavioral response
I find it difficult to work as a team.	Frustration, confusion.	I should have scored. I don't need any help.	When I tried to score the goal on my own, I missed the chance.	The coach explained to me that teamwork and sharing the ball is important for the success of the team.	Teamwork is important for the success of the team. I can trust my teammates and share.	Listen to my teammates and try to include them in the game. Practice sharing and work better with my team.

Identifying the situation:

Identify specific situations where they feel the need to do things on their own, without taking the team into account.

Feelings:

Write down their feelings during these situations.

Automatic thoughts:

Identify their immediate thoughts that may hinder effective teamwork.

Evidence supporting these thoughts:

Identify why they made these thoughts.

Evidence against these thoughts:

Think about why these thoughts may be false.

Alternative thoughts:

Develop positive and constructive thoughts to replace negative ones.

Behavioral response:

Plan specific actions they can take to improve their teamwork and cooperation skills.

35

Dealing with rejection or failure

In a similar situation:

Accept your feelings: It is normal to feel sad and disappointed. You can say to yourself, "It's okay to feel this way. Let me give myself some time to calm down."

Talk about how you feel: Talk to a friend, parent or teacher about your feelings. Say "I feel disappointed that I didn't get the solo, but I want to talk about it so I can feel better."

Think about the process, not the outcome: Acknowledge the effort you put in and how much you improved. Think "Even though I didn't get the solo, I learned a lot and got better."

Set new goals: Think about what you can improve and set new goals for the future. Say "I will work hard and try again for the next solo".

Keep participating: Don't let disappointment keep you from participating in choir. Think "Choir is an opportunity to improve with my friends."

See rejection as an opportunity to learn: Use the experience to learn and improve. Say "This experience is helping me become stronger and more determined."

Story

Emma has practiced for weeks to get a solo in the school choir, but when the results are posted, her name is not on the list. Feeling devastated, she cannot hold her tears and refuses to participate in the choir. Her teacher sits down with her, explaining that everyone faces rejection and that it's an opportunity to learn and improve.

- Have you ever felt as frustrated by rejection as Emma did? How did you react?
- How do you think Emma could have handled her feelings after the rejection?
- What would you do if you were in Emma's shoes and your teacher told you that rejection is an opportunity to learn and improve?

35

Objectives:	Activities:

#1
Understanding and managing rejection

Understand that rejection is part of life and learn ways to manage it.

- **Discuss rejection:** Discuss different examples of rejection and how they can lead to personal growth and improvement.
- **Reflection exercise:** Ask the adolescent to write or talk about a past experience of rejection and how they overcame their feelings.

#2
Developing resilience and perseverance

Enhance resilience and learn to persevere despite disappointments.

- **Talk about resilience:** Discuss what resilience means and how the adolescent can persevere in difficult situations.
- **Resilience exercises:** Create exercises to help the adolescent develop resilience, such as setting small goals and monitoring their progress.

#3
Improving self-esteem

Improve self-esteem and recognize self-worth regardless of rejections.

- **Talk about self-esteem:** Discuss the importance of self-esteem and how the adolescent can strengthen it.
- **Strengths recognition exercise:** Ask the adolescent to write down their positive traits and abilities and acknowledge them.

#4
Developing communication and expressive skills

Learn to express feelings in a healthy way and communicate concerns.

- **Talk about expressing emotions:** Discuss how the adolescent can express their emotions in a healthy way and why it's important.
- **Emotions journal:** Encourage the adolescent to keep a journal recording their feelings and how they manage them.

#5
Developing improvement strategies

Identify opportunities for improvement and develop strategies to achieve goals.

- **Talk about opportunities for improvement:** Discuss how rejection can be an opportunity to improve and set new goals.
- **Action plan:** Create an action plan together with specific steps to help the adolescent improve their skills.

#6
Strengthening participation and cooperation in the group

Commit to the success of the group and learn to work with peers despite frustrations.

- **Talk about collaboration:** Discuss the importance of teamwork and how each member contributes to the success of the group.
- **Group activities:** Provide activities that will enhance the adolescent's cooperation and participation skills, such as group games and rehearsals.

Situation	Feelings	Automatic thoughts	Evidence supporting these thoughts	Evidence against these thoughts	Alternative thoughts	Behavioral response
When I fail at something I can't deal with it.	Disappointment, sadness, anger	I'm not good enough. I will never make it.	I didn't make it even though I tried very hard.	My teacher told me that everyone experiences rejection and that it was an opportunity to learn and improve.	Rejection is an opportunity to learn and improve. I can work harder and try again.	Keep working and try harder for the next opportunity. Ask for help on how to improve and practice on my weaknesses.
_____	_____	_____	_____		_____	_____
_____	_____	_____	_____		_____	_____
_____	_____	_____	_____		_____	_____
_____	_____	_____	_____		_____	_____
_____	_____	_____	_____		_____	_____
_____	_____	_____	_____		_____	_____
_____	_____	_____				_____
_____						

Identifying the situation:

Identify specific situations where they feel frustrated by rejection.

Feelings:

Write down their feelings during these situations.

Automatic thoughts:

Identify their immediate thoughts that may prevent them from accepting rejection as an opportunity for learning.

Evidence supporting these thoughts:

Identify why they made these thoughts.

Evidence against these thoughts:

Think about why these thoughts may be false.

Alternative thoughts:

Develop positive and constructive thoughts to replace negative ones.

Behavioral response:

Plan specific actions they can take to improve their skills and deal with rejection more constructively.

36

Work environment

Useful tips

In a similar situation:

Understand the constructive criticism: Consider that criticism is meant to help you improve, not to insult you. Think "My supervisor's criticism is about getting better at my job."

Listen carefully: When receiving criticism, listen carefully without interrupting. Say "Thank you for the feedback. I will try to work on it."

Ask for clarification if needed: If you don't understand the criticism, ask for more information. Say "Can you explain how I can improve making coffee?"

Keep your temper: Try to remain calm and not take the criticism personally. Think "This criticism is to improve my skills, not to frustrate me."

Respond professionally: Don't walk away when you receive criticism. Instead, say "I will work on this and improve. Thanks for the guidance."

Use criticism to learn: Use criticism as a learning tool to improve your skills. Think "I will use these comments to get better at making coffee".

Story

In his first job in a coffee shop, Ben struggles with the fast pace. When his supervisor comments on his coffee-making skills, Ben takes it personally and gets upset. He doesn't know how to react and simply walks away, leaving his work unfinished. Later, a colleague explains to him the importance of accepting constructive criticism and responding professionally.

- Have you ever felt upset by comments you received about your work, like Ben? How did you respond?
- How would you react if you were in Ben's position and your supervisor made comments about your abilities?
- What do you think Ben could have done to better receive the criticism?

36 | |

#1

Understanding and accepting constructive criticism

Learn to understand and accept constructive criticism without taking it personally.

- **Discussion on constructive criticism:** Explain what constructive criticism is and how it can help with personal and professional growth.
- **Examples of criticism:** Give examples of positive and constructive criticism and discuss how the adolescent might respond.

#2

Developing emotion management skills

Develop strategies to manage their emotions when under criticism or pressure.

- **Breathing and relaxation exercises:** Teach the adolescent breathing and relaxation exercises that they can use when they feel stressed or upset.
- **Emotions journal:** Encourage the adolescent to keep a journal for recording their feelings and how they manage them.

#3

Developing communication skills

Learn to communicate effectively with supervisors and colleagues.

- **Talk about communication:** Discuss the importance of communication in the workplace and how to express concerns or needs in a professional manner.
- **Role-playing:** Role-play situations where the adolescent has to respond to various situations, such as accepting criticism or asking for help.

#4

Developing work performance skills

Improve coffee making skills and adapt to the fast pace of the cafeteria.

- **Practice:** Provide additional practice for the adolescent to improve their techniques.
- **Colleagues' advice:** Encourage the adolescent to seek advice and guidance from more experienced colleagues.

#5

Developing resilience and perseverance

Develop resilience and perseverance in the face of challenges and difficult situations.

- **Talk about resilience:** Discuss what resilience means and how it can help the adolescent cope with challenges at work.
- **Resilience exercises:** Create exercises to help them develop their resilience, such as setting small goals and monitoring their progress.

#6

Acquiring professional behavior

Learn to behave professionally even in difficult situations.

- **Talk about professional behavior:** Discuss what professional behavior means and how to apply it to different situations.
- **Role-playing:** Role-play situations where the adolescent has to deal with difficult situations in a professional manner, such as managing customer complaints or dealing with pressure at work.

Treatment plan

Situation	Feelings	Automatic thoughts	Evidence supporting these thoughts	Evidence against these thoughts	Alternative thoughts	Behavioral response
When my supervisor made comments about my skills, I didn't know how to react and just walked away. _____ _____ _____ _____ _____ _____ _____	Frustration, disappoint-ment. _____ _____ _____ _____ _____ _____ _____	I'm not good at my job. I will never make it. _____ _____ _____ _____ _____ _____	My supervisor made comments about my skills. _____ _____ _____ _____ _____ _____	My colleague explained to me the importance of receiving constructive criticism and responding professionally	Criticism is an opportunity to improve. I can learn and become better. _____ _____ _____ _____	Ask the supervisor for clarification on how to improve. Approach comments with a positive attitude and see what I can learn from them. _____

Identifying the situation:

Identify specific situations where they feel upset because of criticism.

Feelings:

Write down their feelings during these situations.

Automatic thoughts:

Identify their immediate thoughts that may prevent them from accepting criticism.

Evidence supporting these thoughts:

Identify why they made these thoughts.

Evidence against these thoughts:

Think about why these thoughts may be false.

Alternative thoughts:

Develop positive and constructive thoughts to replace negative ones.

Behavioral response:

Plan specific actions they can take to improve their reactions to criticism and develop their skills.

37

Planning and hosting social events

Useful tips

In a similar situation:

Make a list: Make a list of everything you need, such as snacks, drinks and games. Think "What do we need to have fun? I'll make a list so I don't forget anything."

Prepare snacks and refreshments: Buy or make snacks and drinks before guests arrive. Think "I'll make snacks early so I'll be ready when my friends arrive."

Set up the games beforehand: Make sure the games are ready. Think "I'll set up the games before the guests arrive so we can get started right away."

Guide your guests: When your friends arrive, guide them on what you're going to do. Say "Come on, everything is ready. What do you want to play first?"

Communicate expectations clearly: Before the event, let your friends know what to expect. Say "We'll have snacks and play board games. I can't wait to see you!"

Stay flexible and calm: If something doesn't go as planned, try to stay calm and flexible. Think "If everything doesn't go as planned, we'll adjust and find something else to do."

Story

When Elijah decides to host a game night at his house, he is excited but doesn't know how to plan it. He invites friends but forgets to prepare snacks or organize games. When the guests arrive, they look confused and bored, causing Elijah to feel nervous.

- Have you ever organized something and felt irritated because it didn't go as you expected?
- How would you feel if your guests were confused and bored at an event you planned?
- What would you do differently next time to better prepare for a game night you're hosting?

37

| Objectives: | Activities: |

#1

Understanding the importance of event planning

Learn the importance of planning and organizing for the success of an event.

- **Talk about planning:** Explain the key elements needed to plan a successful event, such as preparing snacks and organizing activities.
- **Creating a list:** Help the adolescent create a list of everything they need to prepare for game night, such as snacks, drinks, games, and decorations.

#2

Developing organizational and scheduling skills

Develop organizational skills and learn to manage time effectively.

- **Create a schedule:** Help the adolescent create a schedule to host a game night, including shopping, preparation, and decorating.
- **Organizing activities:** Help them decide which games to play and how to organize them so that guests have a fun experience.

#3

Developing hospitality skills

Learn how to be a good host and ensure that guests are comfortable and entertained.

- **Talk about hospitality:** Discuss the basics of hospitality, such as welcoming guests, offering snacks, and keeping them engaged.
- **Practice hospitality:** Pretend to be a guest and help the adolescent practice how to welcome guests, offer snacks,, and organize activities.

#4

Developing social and anger management skills

Learn how to manage anger and develop social skills for better interaction with guests.

- **Talk about anger management:** Discuss anger management techniques and how to stay calm when things don't go as planned.
- **Social skills exercises:** Practice social interaction scenarios, such as how to initiate conversations and keep guests interested.

#5

Developing communication skills

Learn to communicate effectively with guests and respond to their needs during the event.

- **Talk about communication:** Discuss the importance of communication during the event and how to ask guests if they need anything.
- **Communication practice:** Role-play situations where the adolescent must respond to various situations, such as guests asking for help or having other questions.

Situation	Feelings	Automatic thoughts	Evidence supporting these thoughts	Evidence against these thoughts	Alternative thoughts	Behavioral response
When I invited my friends to my home I was excited, but I didn't know how to plan it. The guests looked confused and it made me nervous. _____ _____ _____	Stress, nervousness, disappoint-ment. _____ _____ _____ _____ _____ _____ _____	My friends don't have fun. It was a mistake to invite them. _____ _____ _____ _____ _____ _____ _____	The guests looked confused and bored. _____ _____ _____ _____ _____ _____ _____ _____	On other occasions, when I had planned the event better, the guests were entertained. _____ _____ _____	I can improve my organizationa l skills. My friends are here to have a good time, not to judge me. _____ _____	Prepare a list of things needed before the next game night. Ask my friends for suggestions and involve them in the planning. _____ _____

Identifying the situation:

Identify specific situations where they feel frustrated and disappointed due to their poor organization skills.

Feelings:

Write down their feelings during these situations.

Automatic thoughts:

Identify their immediate thoughts that may prevent them from effectively planning an event.

Evidence supporting these thoughts:

Identify why they made these thoughts.

Evidence against these thoughts:

Think about why these thoughts may be false.

Alternative thoughts:

Develop positive and constructive thoughts to replace negative ones.

Behavioral response:

Plan specific actions they can take to improve their planning skills and make game nights more pleasant for the guests.

38

Respecting personal and cultural boundaries

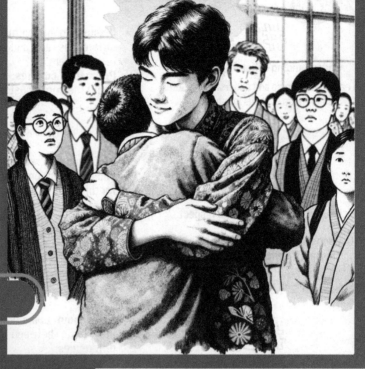

Useful tips

In a similar situation:

Learn the cultural rules: Before you greet your new classmates, find out how they like to greet in their country. Think "Is it better to shake hands or just say hello?"

Observe others' reactions: If you notice that someone is uncomfortable with a hug, adjust accordingly. Think "I'll watch how they react and adjust if necessary."

Ask about their preferences: If you're not sure how to greet, ask politely. Say "How do you prefer to greet?"

Be open to explanations: If someone reacts strangely or seems uncomfortable, you can ask subtly if you did something wrong. That way, you'll learn what to avoid in the future. Say something like " It looks like you feel uncomfortable, did I do something wrong?"

Be kind and patient: If others don't understand your habits, explain them politely. You can say "I'm sorry if I made you uncomfortable."

Talk to an adult you trust: If you ever feel confused or uncomfortable because of a cultural difference, talk to a teacher, parent, or other trusted adult. They can give you advice and help you better understand the situation.

Story

During a student exchange program, George tries to welcome his new foreign classmates. He greets them all with a hug, not realizing that this makes some students uncomfortable because of their cultural habits. Confused by their reactions, George feels uncomfortable. His teacher later explains to him the importance of recognizing and respecting cultural differences in social interactions.

- Why did George feel uncomfortable?
- Why did his new classmates feel uncomfortable when he greeted them with a hug?
- What did George learn from his teacher about cultural differences and social interactions?

38

Objectives:	Activities:

#1

Understanding cultural differences

Learn to recognize and understand cultural differences in social interactions.

- **Discussion on cultural differences:** Explain what cultural differences are and why it's important to recognize and respect them.
- **Presenting cultures:** Ask the adolescent to research and talk about the social customs and traditions of different cultures.

#2

Developing sensitivity and respect

Develop the ability to show sensitivity and respect for others' cultural habits.

- **Discussion on respect:** Discuss the importance of respect in social interactions and how the adolescent can show respect for different cultural customs.
- **Role-playing:** Role-play situations where the adolescent has to interact with people from different cultures, showing respect for their customs.

#3

Developing communication and adaptability skills

Learn to communicate and adapt to different social and cultural situations.

- **Talk about communication:** Discuss how communication may differ between cultures and how to adapt to these differences.
- **Practice communication:** Practice scenarios where the adolescent must communicate with people from different cultures, adjusting their behavior accordingly.

#4

Strengthening empathy and understanding

Develop the ability to understand and show empathy for others' feelings and reactions.

- **Discussion on Empathy:** Discuss what empathy means and how the adolescent can use it in their social interactions.
- **Comprehension exercises:** Role-play situations where the adolescent has to recognize and respond to the feelings of others, understanding their reactions.

#5

Developing social sensitivity skills

Develop social sensitivity and learn how to interact respectfully in multicultural environments.

- **Discussion on social sensitivity:** Discuss the importance of social sensitivity and how the adolescent can be more mindful in their social interactions.
- **Multicultural sensitivity exercises:** Organize activities that will help the adolescent become familiar with different cultures and develop respect for different social customs.

38

Treatment plan

Situation	Feelings	Automatic thoughts	Evidence supporting these thoughts	Evidence against these thoughts	Alternative thoughts	Behavioral response
Sometimes in my attempt to be friendly I make others uncomfortable. ___ ___ ___ ___ ___ ___ ___ ___	Discomfort, confusion, disappointment. ___ ___ ___ ___ ___ ___ ___ ___ ___	The others don't like me. I did something wrong. ___ ___ ___ ___ ___ ___ ___ ___	The others reacted surprisingly to my behavior. ___ ___ ___ ___ ___ ___ ___	This is because of cultural differences, not because they don't like me. ___ ___ ___ ___ ___	I can learn about cultural differences and adapt my behavior. Accepting others does not only depend on a gesture. ___ ___	Ask my classmates about their cultural habits and adapt my behavior accordingly. Find more acceptable ways to greet people. ___

Identifying the situation:

Identify specific situations where their actions may cause misunderstandings.

Feelings:

Write down their feelings during these situations.

Automatic thoughts:

Identify their immediate thoughts that may prevent them from understanding the real cause of the reactions of others.

Evidence supporting these thoughts:

Identify why they made these thoughts.

Evidence against these thoughts:

Think about why these thoughts may be false.

Alternative thoughts:

Develop positive and constructive thoughts to replace negative ones.

Behavioral response:

Plan specific actions they can take to adapt their behavior and show respect for cultural differences.

39

Self-advocacy and expression of personal needs

Useful tips

In a similar situation:

Be prepared: Think about what bothers you and how you can express it before it happens. For example, if noise bothers you, you can say "Can we work in a quieter place?"

Use simple phrases: Use simple and short phrases to express your needs. Say something like, "The noise bothers me. I need quiet to concentrate."

Talk to a teacher or counselor: Tell your teacher or a school counselor how you feel in these situations. They can help you find solutions and explain your needs to your classmates.

Use non-verbal ways of communicating: If you have difficulty expressing yourself verbally, you can use message cards or a notebook to write down what you need (e.g., "I need more quiet").

Give explanations after the situation: If you leave abruptly because of noise, you can explain later to your classmates what happened. Say something like "I'm sorry I left suddenly, the noise was too loud for me."

Work with the group for solutions: Talk with your team about ways that can help you feel more comfortable. Perhaps you can find a quiet place or use headphones to reduce noise.

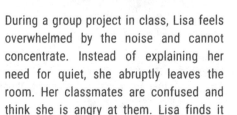

Story

During a group project in class, Lisa feels overwhelmed by the noise and cannot concentrate. Instead of explaining her need for quiet, she abruptly leaves the room. Her classmates are confused and think she is angry at them. Lisa finds it difficult to express her needs clearly, resulting in misunderstandings.

- Why did Lisa feel overwhelmed during group project work in class?
- How did Lisa's classmates react when she abruptly left the room? Why were they confused?
- What could Lisa have done to better express her needs?

Objectives:	Activities:

#1

Developing self-awareness skills

Learn to recognize and understand their feelings and needs in different situations.

- **Discussion on self-awareness:** Explain the meaning of self-awareness and why it is important. Ask the adolescent to record when they feel uncomfortable and why.
- **Emotions journal:** Encourage the adolescent to keep an emotions journal where they record how they feel in different situations and what helps them feel better.

#2

Developing communication skills

Learn to express their needs and feelings clearly to classmates and teachers.

- **Talk about communication:** Discuss the importance of communication and how to express their needs clearly and politely.
- **Role-playing:** Role-play situations where the adolescent has to ask for a quieter place or explain how they feel when there is noise in the classroom.

#3

Developing stress management and sensory sensitivity skills

Develop strategies for managing anxiety and sensory sensitivity in disrupting environments.

- **Talk about stress management:** Discuss techniques for managing anxiety and how they can be applied to noisy situations.
- **Relaxation exercises:** Teach relaxation exercises such as deep breathing or using headphones with music to block out noise.

#4

Developing problem-solving skills

Learn to identify problems and find ways to solve them without running away from the situation.

- **Talk about problem-solving:** Discuss how to identify problems and think of possible solutions.
- **Problem-solving exercises:** Give the adolescent different scenarios and ask them to come up with solutions on how they could deal with situations that bother them, such as noise in the classroom.

#5

Strengthening social skills and understanding

Develop social skills and understand the reactions of others when expressing their needs.

- **Discussion on social skills:** Discuss the importance of social skills and how to apply them to their interactions.
- **Social skills exercises:** Practice scenarios where the adolescent has to interact with their classmates, express their needs, and understand their reactions.

Situation	Feelings	Automatic thoughts	Evidence supporting these thoughts	Evidence against these thoughts	Alternative thoughts	Behavioral response
Sometimes I feel overwhelmed by the noise and can't concentrate. Instead of explaining my need, I leave the room.	Anxiety, withdrawal, nervousness.	I can't concentrate. The others won't understand me.	The noise made me feel stressed and unable to concentrate. I left and the others were confused.	When I explained my needs in other situations, people were understanding.	I can explain my need for quiet in a calm way. My classmates will be supportive if I'm honest.	Clearly express my need for a quieter place before I get to the point of feeling overwhelmed.

Identifying the situation:

Identify specific situations where they feel overwhelmed and cannot concentrate.

Feelings:

Write down their feelings during these situations.

Automatic thoughts:

Identify their immediate thoughts that may prevent them from dealing effectively with the situation.

Evidence supporting these thoughts:

Identify why they made these thoughts.

Evidence against these thoughts:

Think about why these thoughts may be false.

Alternative thoughts:

Develop positive and constructive thoughts to replace negative ones.

Behavioral response:

Plan specific actions they can take to improve the expression of their needs and avoid misunderstandings.

40

New social environments

Useful tips

In a similar situation:

Start with a greeting: When you see a group of students, try saying a simple "hello." This can be a good first step to start a conversation and show that you're open for a friendly conversation.

Look for common interests: Observe what other students are doing and if you find something in common, you can start a conversation around it. For example, if you see that they are reading a book you like, you can say "I like that book too!"

Participate in activities: If there are group activities during recess, such as games or workshops, try to participate. This is a good way to get to know other students with common interests.

Use the help of a teacher: Talk to a teacher and explain how you feel. Teachers can introduce you to other students or give you advice on how to fit in.

Take one small step at a time: Don't expect to join a large group right away. Start by getting to know one or two students and slowly you will become more comfortable.

Express yourself with confidence: Try not to hesitate to reach out to others. Try to be open-minded and try not to shy away from people. Say something like "Hi, can I sit with you? I'm new and don't know anyone yet." Most students will appreciate your honesty and will welcome you.

Story

When Natalie starts at a new school, she feels lost during recess. She doesn't know anyone and isn't sure how to join a group. She sits alone, feeling anxious and excluded.

- Why did Natalie feel lost during recess at her new school?
- What emotions did Natalie feel when she sat alone?
- What could Natalie do to feel more comfortable at her new school?
- Have you ever been in a similar situation? What did you do?

#1

Understanding and managing stress in new social environments

Learn to recognize and manage stress arising from new social environments.

- **Talk about anxiety:** Explain what anxiety is and how it can arise in unfamiliar situations, such as when starting at a new school.
- **Relaxation exercises:** Teach relaxation techniques, such as deep breathing and meditation, that they can practice when they feel stressed.

#2

Developing social skills and integration strategies

Learn strategies to integrate into groups and develop social skills.

- **Discussion on social skills:** Discuss the importance of social skills and how they can develop them.
- **Role-playing:** Role-play situations where the adolescent has to approach other students and talk to them. Practice phrases and ways to start a conversation.

#3

Creating opportunities for social interaction

Develop the ability to create opportunities for social interaction.

- **Talk about interaction opportunities:** Discuss different ways in which the adolescent can create opportunities to join groups, such as participating in games or activities.
- **Participate in group activities:** Encourage participation in group activities that match their interests.

#4

Developing communication and expressive skills

Learn to express their feelings and communicate their needs clearly.

- **Talk about communication:** Discuss the importance of communication and how to express their feelings and needs.
- **Communication exercises:** Provide opportunities for them to practice communicating with classmates, such as asking to participate in activities or explaining how they feel.

#5

Understanding and developing empathy

Develop the ability to understand and respond to the feelings of others.

- **Talk about empathy:** Discuss what empathy is and how it can help develop relationships with others.
- **Empathy exercises:** Role-play situations where the adolescent must recognize the feelings of others and respond with understanding and respect.

#6

Developing self-esteem and self-confidence

Boost their self-esteem and self-confidence so that they feel more comfortable in social interactions.

- **Discuss self-esteem:** Discuss what self-esteem is and how it can be strengthened.
- **Strengths recognition exercise:** Ask the adolescent to list their strengths and positive qualities and discuss how these can help them feel more comfortable in social situations.

40

Treatment plan

Situation	Feelings	Automatic thoughts	Evidence supporting these thoughts	Evidence against these thoughts	Alternative thoughts	Behavioral response
I started in a new school and I feel lost because I don't know anyone and I'm not sure how to join a group. ___ ___ ___ ___ ___ ___	Stress, exclusion, loneliness. ___ ___ ___ ___ ___ ___ ___ ___	I don't know anyone. They will not accept me into their circle. ___ ___ ___ ___ ___ ___	I was sitting alone and no one came to talk to me. I have no friends here. ___ ___ ___ ___ ___	There are other new students who probably feel the same way. I have made friends in the past in other environments	I can take the first step and approach someone. I can find someone who seems friendly and start a conversation. ___ ___ ___	Approach someone and introduce myself. Participate in activities or groups that interest me. ___ ___ ___ ___ ___

Identifying the situation:

Identify specific situations where they feel lost or excluded.

Feelings:

Write down their feelings during these situations.

Automatic thoughts:

Identify their immediate thoughts that may hinder social integration.

Evidence supporting these thoughts:

Identify why they made these thoughts.

Evidence against these thoughts:

Think about why these thoughts may be false.

Alternative thoughts:

Develop positive and constructive thoughts to replace negative ones.

Behavioral response:

Plan specific actions they can take to improve their social integration and friendships.

Made in the USA
Las Vegas, NV
02 January 2025

15674723R00072